D1000252

# FABERGÉ

# FABERGÉ

## KAREN FARRINGTON

Thunder Bay
P·R·E·S·S

Page two: Fabergé's Apple Blossom Easter Egg, please see page 38

ACKNOWLEDGEMENTS

The publisher wishes to thank Christie's Images, who kindly supplied most of the photograhps for this book.
The photographs on page 12-13, 14, 115, 16, 122-123, 124 appear courtesy of Corbis/The Historical Picture
Archive. The picture on pages 30-31 appears courtesy of Corbis/Kelly-Mooney Photography. The picture
on pages 60-61 appears courtesy of Corbis/Michael Freeman. The picture on page 141 appears courtesy of
Corbis and is reproduced by permission of the State Hermitage Museum, Saint Petersburg, Russia.

This edition published in 1999 by
Thunder Bay Press
5880 Oberlin Drive, Suite 400
San Diego, California 92121
1-800-284-3580

http://www.advmkt.com

Produced by PRC Publishing Ltd,
Kiln House, 210 New Kings Road, London SW6 4NZ

© 1999 PRC Publishing Ltd

ISBN 1 57145 203 6

1 2 3 4 5 98 99 00 01 02

Printed and bound in China

# CONTENTS

FOR THE LOVE OF PRECIOUS METALS

**FOR THE LOVE OF PRECIOUS METALS,** men have begged, borrowed, thieved and even killed. The glint of a diamond can ignite consuming passions that transform a reasonable man into a raging fiend. All this because gold, silver and rare stones are endowed with the ability to buy the heart's desires. Yet there is another way to interpret this natural beauty . . .

No one has known a greater devotion to jewels than Carl Fabergé, the esteemed goldsmith who rose to prominence in the twilight years of Imperial rule in Russia. Yet his ardor for such treasures had little to do with their worth or the financial rewards they would bring. For him it was much more than just so much bullion. He found the joy of gems lay in the art forms they could create, given the impetus of clever design. Man joining forces with nature, with sensational results. He inspired the same noble feelings in his customers who yearned to own a Fabergé item not for its cash value, but for its own sake. These highly appealing *objets d'art* were a pleasure to possess.

At times he was extravagant, at times he was frivolous. There were instances where he was positively minimalist. His artwork encompassed the styles of antiquity and Art Nouveau, and almost everything that fell between. Still, the magic of Fabergé runs like an electrical current through his works so that more contemporary pieces can seem lackluster by comparison.

The romance of Fabergé has escalated over the years. His life bridged two ages — opulence and austerity — lending new depths to his story. His conversation was enigmatic and his character almost entirely eclipsed by his creations. Thus, the man who had some of the world's mightiest rulers in his thrall remains as fascinating today as ever.

8

**Previous page:** An enamel and porcelain snuff box with Renaissance-style cherubs.

CARL

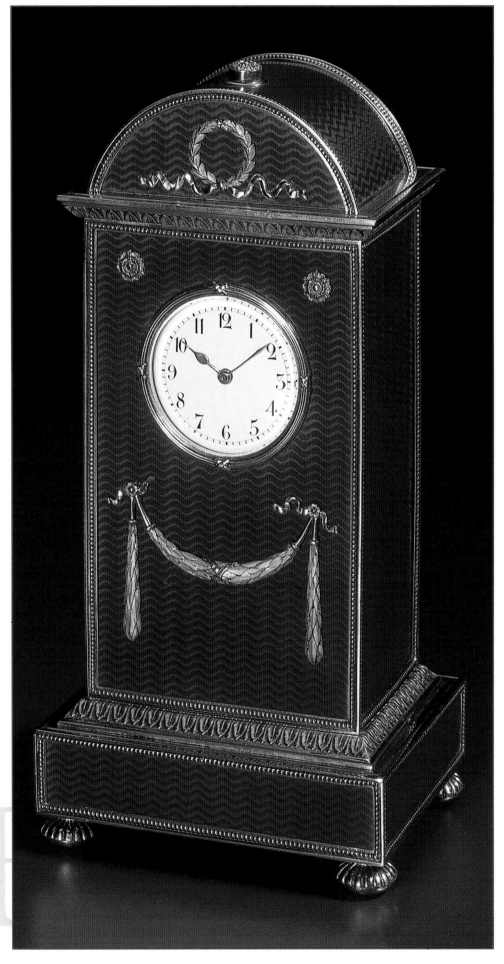

**Left**: A garlanded clock with silver-gilt motifs on a blue *guilloche* enamel background bearing the scratched inventory number 10776.

FA BE

**Right**: Sitting on a three-pronged plinth, this silver table lighter rises from lion's paw feet into a pine cone body. A fluted finial hides the wick.

**Left**: This smoky glass bottle, with its tapering rectangle shape rests on four bun feet. It was made in St Petersburg in about 1900.

# THE MAN

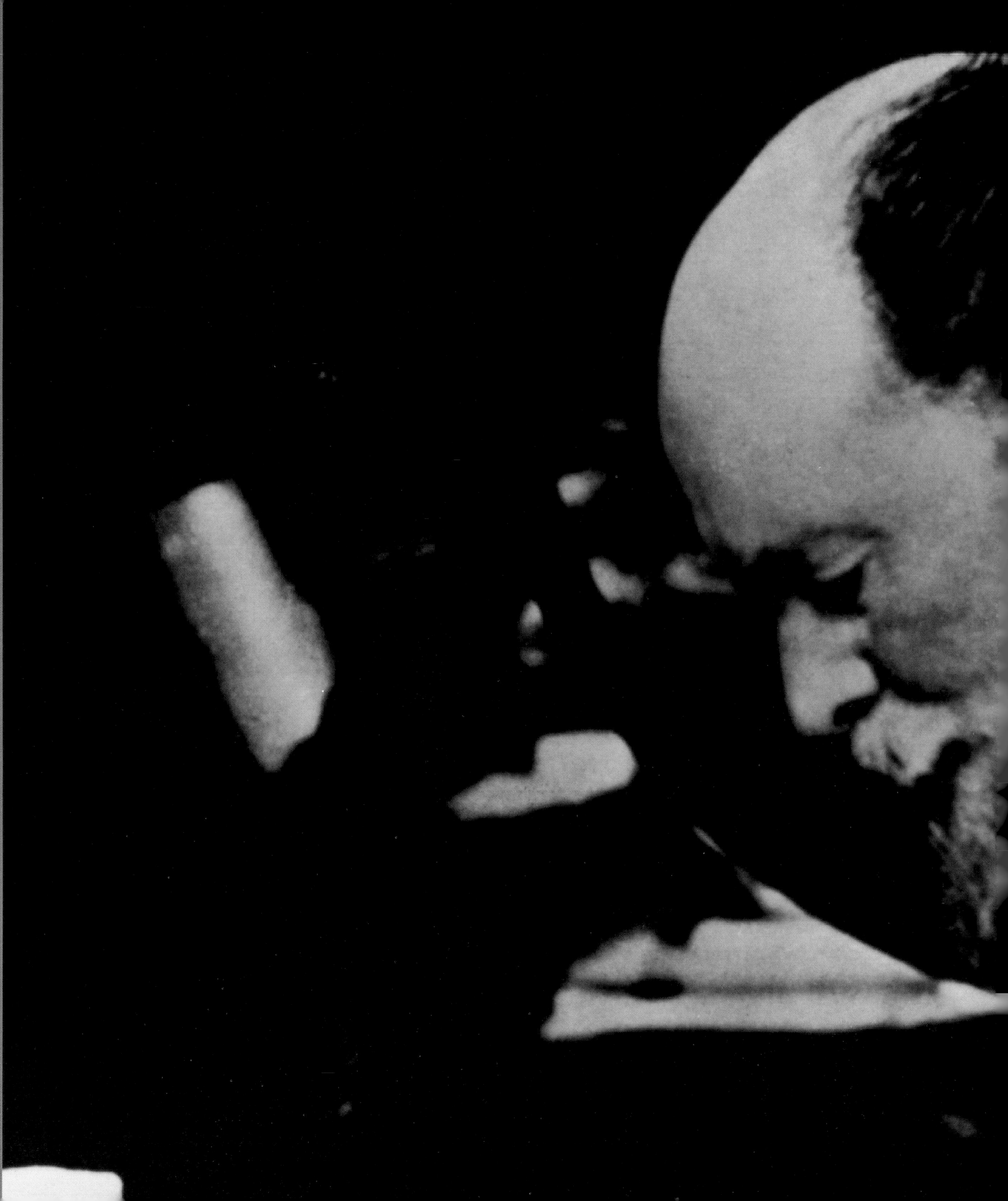

# PETER CARL FABERGÉ

**PETER CARL FABERGÉ was born on May 30, 1846, in St Petersburg, Russia, to jeweler Gustav Fabergé and his Scandanavian bride Charlotte Jungstedt, the daughter of a Danish painter. The family were originally French protestants, hence the Gallic name, and had fled from the religious persecution licensed by Louis XIV in or around 1685. They arrived in Russia by way of Germany.**

**Above**: Fabergé craftsmen often had to use magnifying glasses to carry out the detailed work that each piece demanded.

It was Gustav (1814–91) who opened the first basement shop on Bolshaya Morskaya Street in St Petersburg that would one day be the seat of an empire. He studied the art of jewelry-making under acclaimed experts Andreas Ferdinandas Shpigel and Yorgan William Kibel. Eventually Gustav became known as "The Master of Jewelry." His speciality was diamonds. Yet history saw his successes surpassed by those of his son. When he retired in 1860 Gustav left not only the business, but Russia itself, and headed for Dresden in Germany. His company continued to function under the guidance of his Finnish partner Peter Hiskias Pendin.

Given the travels of his parents Carl Fabergé enjoyed a cosmopolitan education from the Gymnasium Svetaya Anna in St Petersburg and the equally prestigious Hendelschude in Dresden. His schooling was followed by trips to France, England and Italy before he became the apprentice of a jeweler by the name of Joseph Friedmann in Frankfurt. Carl's outlook was thus broad and his cultural experiences significant. The fruits of his time overseas were evident throughout his career as art from bygone ages across the globe influenced his products.

In 1870, he took the reins of the family business, ushering in a new era for the prestigious company — an period that remains clearly recognizable today.

That Fabergé was a master jeweler himself, has never been in doubt. But, had he restricted himself to this task alone the world today would have fewer Fabergé articles in existence. For one man can produce only a limited numbers of artifacts, no matter how hard he works.

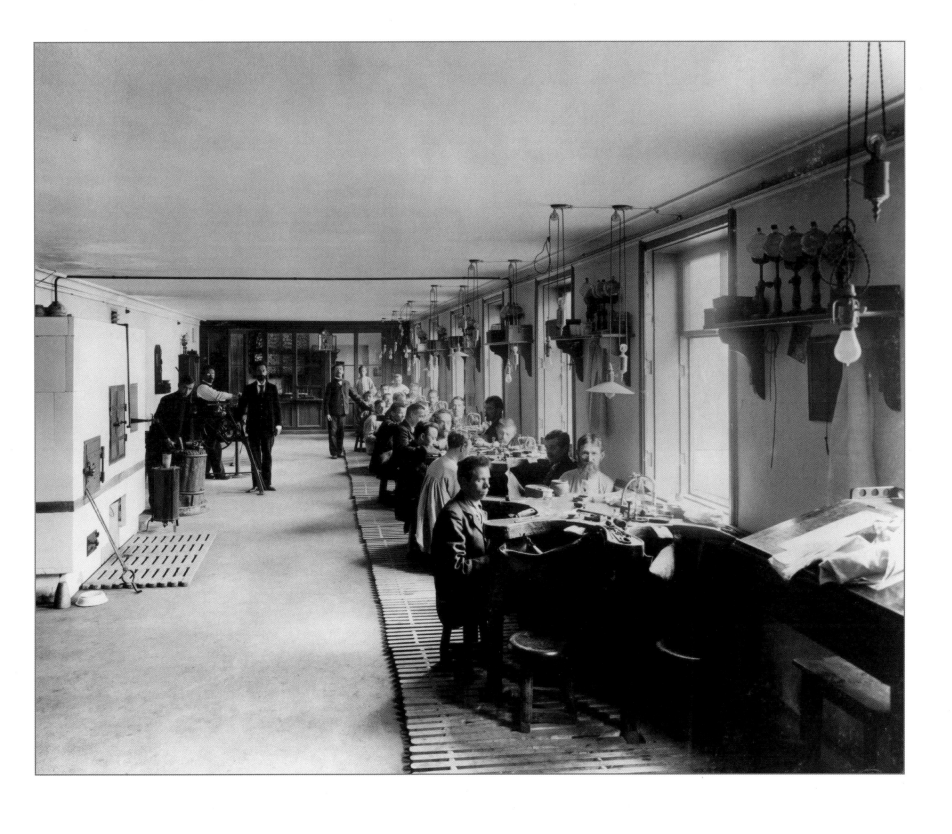

15

**Above**: Although electricity was a valued asset, workmen still relied on the natural light that poured in through large windows to complete their tasks.

**Above and pages 12 to 13:**
Although Peter Carl Fabergé was an entrepreneur first and foremost he maintained an abiding interest in design and always insisted on high standards of workmanship.

Fabergé took a different approach. He approved all designs before they were begun, designing some items himself — but never personally worked on them. This task he entrusted to workmasters whom he fostered by offering rent-free premises and by providing the materials they needed. There were up to two dozen workmasters, each with their own assistants and staff, when Fabergé was at the height of his success.

The finished products were (usually) embellished with the mark of Fabergé, by which they could subsequently be identified. However, it was never his intention to steal the thunder of these other talented workers. Fabergé ensured the most worthy were credited with individual identifiable marks alongside his own. An efficient system was put in place to produce disinctive objects in large quantities.

When his younger brother Agathon, then 20, joined the business in 1882, Carl Fabergé was ably assisted in the realm of design. It was Agathon who was the instinctive artist, able to mimic the styles of the Bourbon kings, the Gothic age and Russian Orthodoxy as well as defining a new expression at the grass roots of the Art Nouveau movement. Like Carl he was sensitive, but there is little else on record about this inspirational man whose sudden death occured before his potential was reached.

Together they decided to scale down the jewelry side of the business and concentrate on *objets d'art*. The same year the Fabergé business won a gold medal at the Pan-Russian exhibition, established as a showcase to display the finest wares Russia could offer the world. The award was in recognition of him "having opened a new era in jewelry art." It was at this exhibition that Fabergé creations first caught the eye of the Empress Marie

and where she purchased the very first artifact of her collection. In fact, Fabergé had already provided great service to the royal couple, although they were probably unaware of it at the time. As a volunteer he worked at the Hermitage, the treasury and museum in the Winter Palace of St Petersburg, where all the Czar's valuables were stored. He cataloged each item, estimated its worth and assisted in repair where necessary.

In 1885, Fabergé was awarded the prestigious title of "Supplier to the Imperial Court" and there was further recognition in 1890 with the accolade "Apprasier of the Imperial Cabinet." While most crown appointees were entitled only to display an imperial crown, Fabergé was permitted to stamp his work with the crowned Imperial eagle, giving his work higher status. There was another gold medal for Fabergé at the 1896 Pan-Russian Exhibition at Nijiny-Novgorod.

The international reputation of the House of Fabergé was sealed in 1900 with a gold medal at the Paris Expostion Universelle. Fabergé created a sensation at this exhibition. French jewelers saw finery reminiscent of all the French kings recreated. British visitors were likewise impressed and one art connoisseur, Leo Davis, called Fabergé, "The last of the great craftsmen." In 1907, Baron A. E.

Foelkersam wrote in his *Inventaire de l'Argenterie* — a catalog of the Czar's luxury possessions — that Fabergé was "the best and most celebrated (firm) in the world."

Helsinki-born August Holmstrom (1829–1903), the chief jeweler appointed by Gustav Fabergé in 1857, was still there when Carl took over, and remained a pivotal presence until his death. His daughter Hilma Alina married another craftsman Knut Pihl (1860–97) and their daughter Alma (1888–1976) designed the 1913 Winter Egg and the 1914 Mosaic Egg.

The other workmasters who rose to prominence in the Fabergé stable were: Finnish goldsmith Erik August Kollin (1836–1901), one of the first to join Fabergé in his venture; Michael Evlampiewitsch Perchin (1860–1903), Kollin's replacement and Henrik Emanuel Wigstrom (1862–1923), who worked in the Fabergé workshop until it was forced to close after the Russia Revolution.

Kollin had a talent for reproducing antiques. It was he who made replicas of treasures fashioned by the nomadic Scythian race before their disappearance in the third century. A trove of Scythian treasure was discovered in the 19th century at Kerch in the Crimea. Alexander III was so impressed by the likenesses that he displayed the originals and the copies side-by-side in the Hermitage to highlight the talent of the goldsmith. It was working with gold at which he excelled. Few of the pieces traced back to Kollin bear the enamel work which is so closely identified with Fabergé. Kollin worked under the Fabergé umbrella for 16 years until 1886 and he died in 1901. His mark engraved alongside the name of Fabergé was "E.K."

**Above:** An ingenious metal table lighter in the form of a monkey with the fuel in the body, accessed through the hinged neck, and the wick emerging from a hollow tail.

**Above**: Rectangular lapis lazuli clock with the face embellished with rose cut diamonds. The silver base plate reads: "To my dearest Phyle, from Bob. Christmas 1924." Outline drawings of the clock found in Henrik Wigstrom's stock book, reveal the item was completed November 26, 1911.

**Opposite page above**: Blue *guilloche* enamel photograph frame marked as the work of workmaster Anders Nevalainen of St Petersburg.

**Opposite page middle**: Rectangular frame surmounted with the imperial crown and containing a miniature of Czar Alexander III as painted by Aleksander Matveevich.

**Opposite page below**: A jeweled blue *guilloche* rectangle enamel frame made by workmaster Hjalmer Armfelt in St Petersburg.

18

Perchin was something of a fairytale figure in late 19th century Russia. He began life as a Russian peasant in Petrozavodsk, at a time when escaping peasant status was nothing short of a Herculean task. Nobody knows where he learned the jeweler's craft but he was sufficiently talented to open his own workshop in 1886. After that he worked exclusively for Fabergé until his death in 1903. It was Perchin who was responsible for making the majority, if not all, of the 19th century Imperial eggs, some 26 in total. His hallmark appears on all eggs made in that period except for the first. So Perchin was a true, "son of the soil," yet he was most comfortable when crafting prized objects for no lesser being than the Czar himself. Apart from the Imperial eggs he made numerous small objects including cigarette cases and writing sets. His style echoed the 18th century Rococo period and that of French King Louis XV. His initials were M.P. (although in the Russian Cyrillic alphabet initials would appear differently). On the death of Perchin, Henrik Wigström took the mantle of chief maker and designer for the Fabergé empire. The hearty, rotund Wigström hailed from the same area of Finland as Kollin. His mark of H.W. is inscribed on items as various as Imperial eggs to flower studies and a wide variety of other curios. His specialties are deemed to be cigarette boxes, frames and figurines. Stylistically, he was most influenced by the era of the French King Louis XVI and the Empire period.

There were other workmasters of note toiling away in St Petersburg. Among them were August Hollming (1854–1913), and his son Vaino (1885–1934), Victor Aarne (1863–1934), enameler Hjalmar Av Armfelt (1873–1959), silversmith Joseph Rappoport, Anders Nevalainen,

Karl Woerffel, Alexander Petroff, as well as craftsmen know only by such surnames as Afanassieff, Niukkanen, Wakawa, Rutsch, Epifanoff, Zahudalin, Pestou, Kremleff, Derbysheff and Boitzoff. Of those listed above, six were Finns, four were Germans and seven were Russian. There were also some women at work, one of the best remembered being the modeler Elena Shishkina.

At its height, the House of Fabergé employed about 500 artisans and had several branches. Moscow's opened in 1887, Odessa's in 1890, another in Kiev opened in 1905 and a year later an outlet in London started up in association with three English brothers, Allan, Arthur and Charles Bowe. The link with the Bowe brothers did not endure as long as Fabergé's trading post in London which began in the city's Berners Hotel, but moved swiftly to Portland House in Grosvenor Square and finally, in 1906, to 48 Dover Street where it remained until 1911. Inside, glass-fronted cabinets illuminated by electric lights, displayed Fabergé wares. Trading in London did not cease until 1917.

Life was hard but satisfying for the workmasters and craftsmen. Typically, they would begin work at 7 am and might not finish until 11 pm although officially the hours were much shorter. On Sundays it was normal to work between 8 am and 1 pm. Still, the atmosphere was not slavish. The men enjoyed good rates of pay for the hours they put in. George Stein, the man employed by Perchin to re-produce the Imperial coronation coach for an Imperial egg later told how he was paid five roubles a day (albeit 16 hours long) instead of three at his previous job. Fabergé attracted craftsmen from all over Russia and Europe with at least five Englishmen being employed in Moscow alone.

According to Dr. Geza von Habsburg, an expert on Fabergé, the workshops offered unique job security, often until employees were beyond pensionable age. There was, he says, a unique *esprit de corps.*

Now Carl had sufficient time to devote to business matters, including marketing and sales, and he became an accomplished entrepreneur. This kind of division of labor was a modern concept which occurred in Russia when it was still trapped in the feudal system. It was efficient and productive, with all those involved reaping rewards.

Yet Fabergé, a man driven by intergrity, refused to compromise on quality. Sloppy workmanship was never tolerated, no matter how great the demand for his items. He would issue the Fabergé hallmark only to the most satisfactory pieces. Those items he considered below standard were destroyed as an issue of quality control. This occured even when Fabergé and all his many workmasters were unable to fulfill the volley of requests for items. Like other things, Fabergé pieces were subject to fashion and even whim. Customers continued to buy in pursuit of the latest ornamental trend.

In a catalog passage published in Moscow in 1899 the Fabergé policy was underlined as:

"We only offer objects which are in perfect condition; this means each item — even if the value is not highter than one rouble — is fabricated with precision in all details.

"We always try — and our customers can always rest assured of it — to offer a large quantity of newly designed articles. Old items which are out of fashion are not kept in stock: once a year they are collected and destroyed.

"We always try to produce our articles in such a way that the value of an object corresponds to the sum of money spent on it, in other words, we are selling our objects as cheaply as the precise execution and workmanship permits.

"Due to our considerable capital we are able to have a stock of a large quantity of articles both in variety and value which are offered to our esteemed customers."

Years later observers are compelled to appreciate the high standards which are so evident throughout the Fabergé collection. Even if one questions the design as being too fancy, too fantastical or simply too bizarre, it is still possible to marvel at the technical brilliance of the piece.

Agathon died in 1895. The circumstances of his passing are a mystery. Swiss jeweler Franz

**Above:** *Cloisonné* enameled birchwood cigarette case with a strutting cockerel and floral scrolls.

Petrovich Birbaum, who joined the company two years previously, was elevated to chief designer to fill the void.

In 1872, Carl Fabergé married Augusta Julia Jacobs, the daughter of the manager of the Czar's furniture workshop, and she bore him four sons, Eugene (1874–1960), Agathon (1876–1951), Alexander (1877–1952) and Nicholas (1884–1939). All would one day join the company although the future they dreamed of, perpetuating Fabergé treasures throughout the 20th century, ended with the onset of revolution.

After the outbreak of the First World War Fabergé and his colleagues were ordered to devote time and materials to making guns and hospital dressings. Any "luxury" items produced by the House of Fabergé at the time were in copper or gunmetal and were stamped with the Russian Imperial eagle and "1914 War."

The war gave way to revolution in Russia where radicals had been active for decades. Nowhere was the gulf between nobility and peasantry greater. First came the Provisional Government comprising Mensheviks and led by Alexander Kerensky, a socialist who found himself in charge of an unwieldy government. Six months later there was another coup, by the Communist Bolsheviks led by Lenin. It was the Bolsheviks with their startling agenda who prevailed.

But the image of Fabergé was at odds with the new Communist regime. A relationship between the two was untenable and life for him and his workers became intolerable.

An estimated 150,000 items had been produced — a colossal number — before the company was forced to close without compensation. When his workshops were shut down (and ransacked) by the Bolsheviks, Fabergé escaped to Switzerland. Deprived of the sizeable organization which had worked like a well-oiled machine under his leadership, Fabergé never worked again.

Away from Russia and the artwork to which he had devoted his life Fabergé faltered and finally failed. He was entirely loyal to Russia and found it hard enough to function well outside his homeland even before his exile. Although his safety was assured in Germany, and later Switzerland, he was often heard to declare, "this is life no more." He died on a September morning, half an hour after smoking his final cigarette.

His sons Eugene and Alexander founded their own Fabergé company in Paris in about 1924 under the name "Fabergé & Cie, Paris" in partnership with others. The rights to the family name was sold by their descendants to American

Sam Rubin in 1951, after he began selling perfumes under the Fabergé name. The company was acquired by Unilever in 1989 and is nowadays best known for its fragrances and aftershaves, although other products include jewelry, glass, silverware and eye glasses.

Fabergé has often been compared to Benvenuto Cellini (1500–71), the goldsmith from Florence recognized as the finest of his era. True, both men were responsible for turning out artwork of excellence, and in doing so, worked for the most prestigious families of their generation. There the similarities end for Cellini was as fiery as Fabergé was reserved. The former gave his opinion freely, the latter used his words wisely. After all, Cellini was thrown out of Florence at the age 16 because of his outbursts of fury and perpetual brawling. In Rome he became a pupil to Michelangelo.

His chief customers were Francis I of France, — for whom he made a fabulous gold salt cellar now in Vienna's Kunsthistoriches Museum — Pope Clement VII, Pope Paul III and the powerful Medici family. With Cosimo de Medici as patron Cellini made the magnificent bronze statue Perseus and Medusa, now housed in Florence.

One of the most valuable works bequeathed to prosperity by Cellini was his autobiography, which not only detailed his escapades and intrigues but shed valuable light on the day-to-day life of Renaissance Italy.

Alas, as far as we know, Fabergé died before penning his life story. His English agent, Henry Charles Bainbridge, made an admirable contribution to all that we know about Fabergé with his 1949 book *Peter Carl Fabergé*. But the author confessed: "To record and pass on the amazing tolerance of the man, his elemental simplicity, in a manner which would make it reasonably certain that a reader could gauge his extraordinary nature, calls for a literary technique and skill which I am far from possessing."

Picture Fabergé using this pen portrait: a man with a tidy beard, usually dressed in tweeds, peering through a magnifying glass to assess minute detail on a fine arts item, his brow furrowed with concentration. He was kind although sarcastic, humorous but also profound. He had a well-honed sense of irony. His economy with words was legendary although he remained convivial company. As von Habsburg said : "Fabergé was full of humor and wit, shy, and self-depracating."

He had a noble air, yet when he traveled to the coronation of Czar Nicholas II through the streets of Moscow in a clapped out coach he was surprised but completely calm when its bottom fell out. He continued the journey cartoon-style, inside the coach with his feet walking along the floor.

There was a lapse of several decades before Fabergé-style items were produced once more. During this time descendents of Fabergé carried out a frustrated search for a center of excellence in the craft of jewelry making. Finally, a German company, Victor Mayer, of Pforzheim, was given official blessing to continue the family tradition and to bear the family crest.

Von Habsburg, even wrote: "The Fabergé workmaster Victor Mayer has succeeded in creating new objects in the spirit of Fabergé which have the right to bear the famous hallmark Fabergé and workmaster mark VM, and are considered by experts as a continuation of the Fabergé tradition."

21

**Above**: A Moscow-made *cloisonné* enamel pill box, less than two inches long, marked as the work of Feodor Ruckert.

**Right**: Silver kettle with a scroll handle and bone centerpiece on a stand with oil burner. Drawing from the St Petersburg workshop.

К. ФАБЕРЖЕ
С.-Петербургъ.

**Left**: A silver table lamp with a twisting, fluted body standing on scroll feet. The watercolor and pencil etching bears the price written in pencil: 250 roubles.

Previous page: A realistically carved bowenite elephant with ruby eyes.

Above: Attributed to Fabergé although apparently unmarked, this stylish square locket has two glazed compartments within.

Opposite page above: A rose cut diamond sits in a circle of gold at the center of this enameled christening cross.

Opposite page below: A gold and *guilloche* enamel thimble made before 1903 in the workshops of August Hollstrom in St Petersburg.

Opposite page far right: A jeweled gold and *guilloche* enamel mounted wood parasol handle from workmaster Henrik Wigström.

26

**A QUESTION STILL BEGS TO BE ASKED. Why was Fabergé so popular and enduring? The answer, says Christie's Russian expert Alexei De Tiesenhausen, lies in the workmanship he displayed:**

"You may like or you may not like Fabergé. Some people find it kitsch. Some people find it crude in style. One thing you cannot criticize is the workmanship. You cannot match it. This is true of big items, small items and everything in the middle. He was also extremely clever at understanding and exploiting the tastes at the time he was producing such items. This was someone with new ideas, who knew how to present them to the public."

Von Habsburg sums it up like this:

"Fabergé items are brilliantly designed, one-of-a-kind, exquisitely crafted and forever part of the tragic story of the last Romanovs.'

Fabergé's work is said variously to sum up the spirit of Russia — the humor, beauty and quirkiness of this sprawling country — and to be quintessentially Edwardian, the era that unfolded during the first decade of the century. Herein was another of his major strengths. Fabergé was one of the few artisans whose fame spread far beyond the Russian borders, even while he was alive.

Edwardian England held a particular affection for all things Fabergé. Bainbridge described it like this:

"Fabergé objects were the outward and visible sign of the spirit of the age. Nothing, whether of importance or of no importance, took place unless signalized by them. The further you departed from Fabergé the less Edwardian you became, the nearer you came to him, the more so you were."

Fabergé had his competitors, both in Russia and abroad. Work by Bolin and Sumin remain highly valued, as does the produce of silversmith Saziqv. Yet no one mastered the range of Fabergé. Outside Russia Fabergé was probably influenced by French jeweler Cartier.

The purity of precious metals was measured in "zolotniks," rather than carats, the measure favored by jewelers in the West. About four zolotniks was equal to one carat which makes 14 carat gold 56 zolotniks, and 18 carat gold 72 zolotniks. The measure for sterling silver was about 91 zolotniks.

Fabergé chose crossed anchors and a sceptre as a hallmark to indicate items that were made in St Petersburg. For Moscow, the symbol was St George and the dragon. Pieces bearing the Imperial double-headed eagle denote those done by royal appointment. After 1896, the Czarist regime insisted that the profile of a woman's head be made the national hallmark. The headdress depicted, and the hallmark itself, were both known as a *kokoshnik*.

However, the marking system was often incomplete. Many genuine Fabergé items bear no identifiable marks while numerous fakes are embellished with the family's name and other familiar symbols.

While 24 carat gold is desirable for making jewelry, it is not sturdy enough for Fabergé-style objects. For this, 14 carat gold was equal to the task. The glitter of yellow gold would have become monotonous for Fabergé so he colored it through the introduction of other metals. Gold mixed with silver gave a green-gold, while gold mixed with

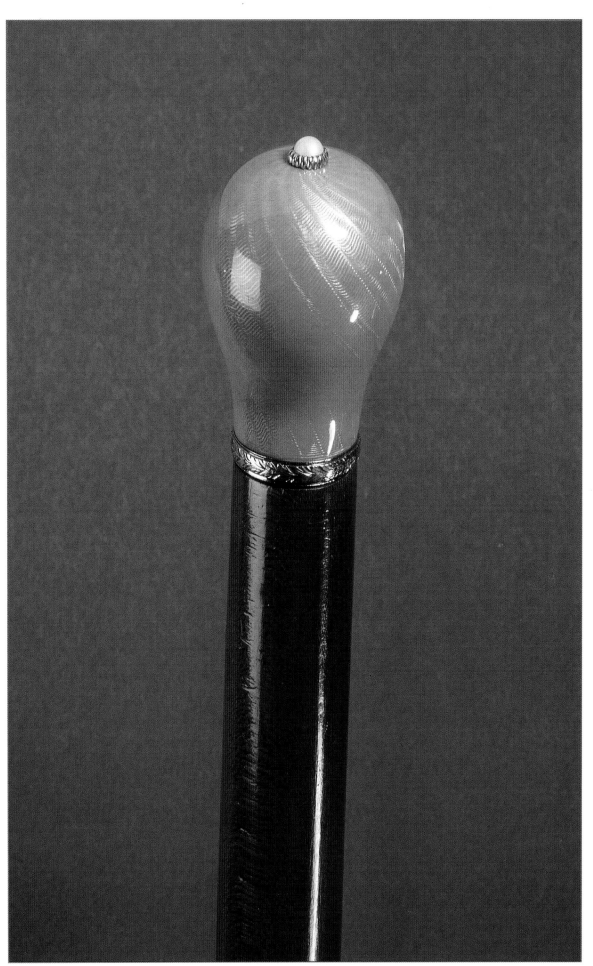

**Above**: Sapphire, ruby and diamond gold brooch made in about 1890.

copper rendered a metallic red metal. Different alloys produced a full spectrum of colors which Fabergé used to his full advantage. He also used another method to distinguish between like-metals, that is the degree to which they were polished.

It was with his work with enamel that Fabergé won plaudits. Enamel is a paste which fuses to metal objects in intense heat. Similar to glass in its chemical structure, the ingredients — silica, sand, soda and lead — are powdered then mixed with oil or water before being applied. The object is then fired in a furnace to make this substance stick. A temperature of around 1,000°C (1,832°F) gives an even finish.

There are various different types of enameling. *Champlevé* enameling is done on an etched metal surface so that the ridges of metal and hollows filled with enamel can be polished at the same time. The *cloisonné* process involves borders that are raised on the metal surface, by soldering strips in place, allowing enamel to fill the gaps. *Basse-Taille* is similar to *champlevé* but this time translucent enamel is used through which designs can be observed. *Plique-á-jour* is the most difficult process to achieve for the enamel stands without the support of a metal object in the same way that a stained-glass window would. Fabergé was not afraid to use this procedure ambitiously, as he was attracted by the light tricks which it could achieve.

However Fabergé's favorite technique was to make a *guilloche* surface in which layers of opaque enamel were fused on to one another. Patterns or scenes might be added during the process before the final layer was fused into place. It was usual to have more than 140 patterns of wavy parallel lines in place before the item was complete. The object was then turned on a wooden wheel and buffed to achieve the quality finish.

As for rocks and stones, Fabergé made wise use of those available within the borders of Russia. These included jasper, rhodonite, the transparent quartz rock crystal, aventurine quartz, lapis lazuli, the deep blue limestone from Siberia or Afghanisatan and agate. Of the two types of jade he made most use of nephrite from Siberia, but occasionally employed jadeite. From India he imported heliotrope, a dark green chalcedony flecked with red.

Of course, he used precious stones including diamonds — mostly rose cut which had the top cut into triangular facets — sapphires, rubies and emeralds. Nevertheless, he was just a likely to turn to less valuable rocks when design dictated, including moonstones, garnets and Mecca stones. Another popular material, pupurine — a dark red stoneglass — was made in factories in St Petersburg.

Yet materials of intrinsic value were not the be all and end all for Fabergé. He'd choose wood rather than gold if the design demanded it. And in addition to silver and precious stones he also worked with pottery, brass, copper, cork and even gun-metal.

Just as he refused to limit himself to one material so he would not be allied to one style. He skipped from the first to the next then on to another, executing each to perfection. He never shied from a challenge but was always ready to tackle the unusual or the off-beat.

**Top left**: Miniature plain yellow metal Easter egg with chased and cast Imperial double-headed eagle from workmaster August Hollming at the turn of the century.

29

**Top right**: Miniature Easter egg from the workmaster Erik Kollin between 1899 and 1903.

**Bottom left**: Attributed to Fabergé this miniature enamel silver and gold Easter egg is thought to have been made in about 1890.

**Bottom right**: Thought to have been made in about 1890 this jewelled plain gold miniature Easter egg is marked as a Fabergé item.

EGGS

ALL OF HIS WORK WAS INNOVATIVE, IMAGINATIVE AND INTRIGUING

**Previous pages:** A Fabergé egg, from the collection of Marjorie Merryweather.

1: This jeweled, gold-mounted bowenite miniature Easter egg with its snake motif is attributed to August Holstrom and was made in about 1912.

2: August Hollming, another workmaster in St Petersburg, was responsible for this mini egg, comprising two *cabochon* moonstones within a diamond, gold-mounted rim.

3: A design inspired by the ice crystals covering the inside of the windows of the Fabergé workshops, it became closely linked to Fabergé customer Emmanuel Nobel. This mini egg is dated through customer records as April 10, 1913.

**ALL OF HIS WORK WAS INNOVATIVE, IMAGINATIVE AND INTRIGUING. Yet nothing has remained so alive in the mind of the public as the Fabergé eggs. For curiosity value alone they have never been exceeded.**

The eggs were created as gifts from the Czar to his wife to mark Easter day. Their faith was Russian Orthodox, an offshoot of the ancient Greek Orthodox Church which split from the Roman Church early in the history of Christianity. The celebration of Easter in Russia is key. On Easter day friends and neighbors greeted one another with three kisses and the words "Christ is risen." Then they exchanged gifts to mark the resurrection. There is, of course, a tradition of decorated eggs being given at Easter as the symbol of new life. Interestingly, it was also the occasion that court officials in Russia could expect to be bribed with gifts or money.

Bainbridge, who worked for Fabergé for 30 years, estimates the year of the first Imperial egg as 1884. Fabergé proposed to make the egg as a gift for the Empress, a seemingly ordinary egg on the outside containing a series of enchanting surprises. Fabergé seized the opportunity to bring his enormous reserves of wit and ingenuity into play. Despite enquiries from the Czar he refused to spoil the wonder of his creation by sharing his secret before Easter arrived.

Says Bainbridge in his biography of Fabergé:

"It was of gold enameled opaque white, and on being opened revealed a yolk also of gold. The yolk opened and inside was a chicken made in gold of different shades. Within the chicken was a model of the Imperial Crown, and inside this hung a tiny ruby egg.

"This pleased the Czar so greatly that he gave the craftsman a standing order for an egg every Easter, and a bargain was struck between Emperor and craftsman. The latter was given a free hand to make whatever took his fancy and the former was to ask no questions, the one stipulation being that each egg must have some surprise inside it.

"But Fabergé's tactics in exciting or kindling the curiosity of his imperial patron were so successful that at last Alexander was unable to keep his pledge and eagerly asked what the next year's surprise was to be. Knowing full well how to speak to princes, the craftsman's only reply was: 'Your Majesty will be content.'"

This first Imperial Easter Egg fetched £85 at an auction by Christie's on March 15, 1934. Today it holds inestimable value.

The eggs themselves were stunning to behold and the subject of countless hours of workmanship. Yet it was the diminutive surprise they contained which rendered them even more remarkable. The least ambitious of the surprises were carefully wrought models of gold embellished with precious stones. The most astonishing were clockwork "toys" which worked perfectly and featured in at least five Fabergé eggs.

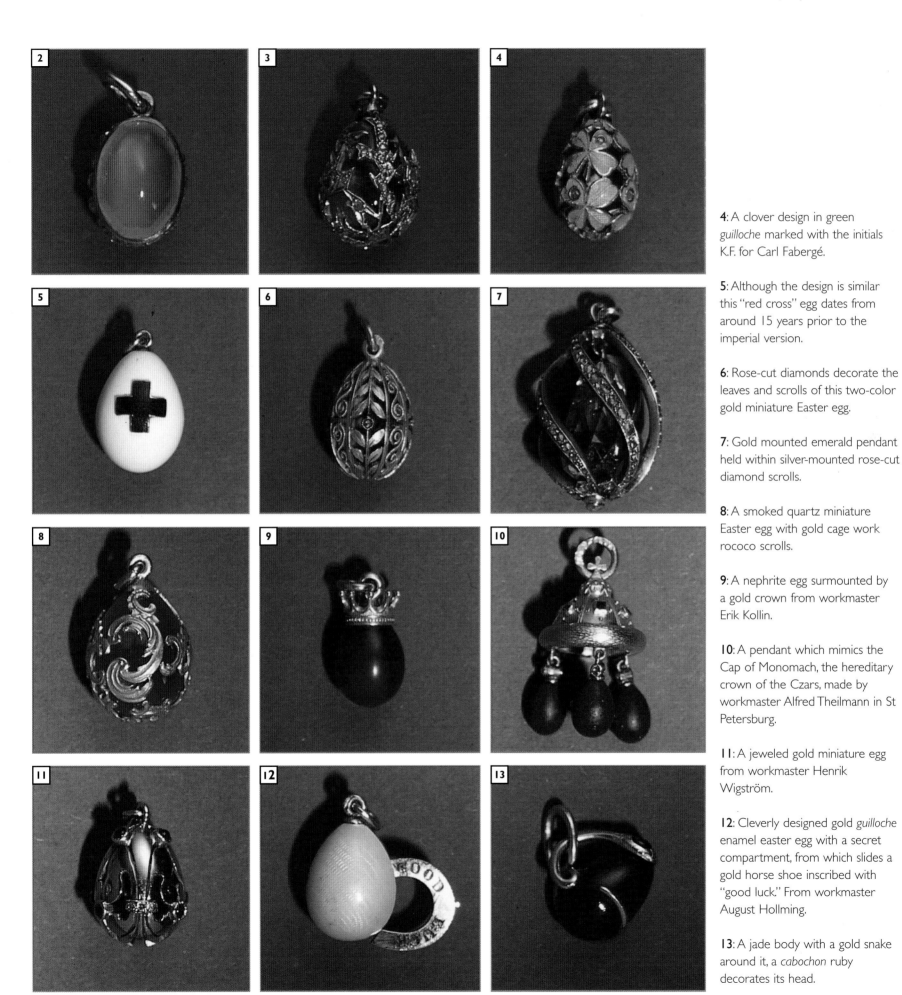

**4**: A clover design in green *guilloche* marked with the initials K.F. for Carl Fabergé.

**5**: Although the design is similar this "red cross" egg dates from around 15 years prior to the imperial version.

**6**: Rose-cut diamonds decorate the leaves and scrolls of this two-color gold miniature Easter egg.

**7**: Gold mounted emerald pendant held within silver-mounted rose-cut diamond scrolls.

**8**: A smoked quartz miniature Easter egg with gold cage work rococo scrolls.

**9**: A nephrite egg surmounted by a gold crown from workmaster Erik Kollin.

**10**: A pendant which mimics the Cap of Monomach, the hereditary crown of the Czars, made by workmaster Alfred Theilmann in St Petersburg.

**11**: A jeweled gold miniature egg from workmaster Henrik Wigström.

**12**: Cleverly designed gold *guilloche* enamel easter egg with a secret compartment, from which slides a gold horse shoe inscribed with "good luck." From workmaster August Hollming.

**13**: A jade body with a gold snake around it, a *cabochon* ruby decorates its head.

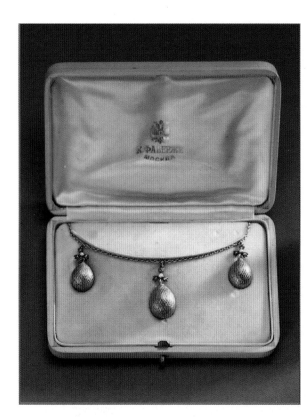

**Above**: Miniature Fabergé eggs became as sought-after as their Imperial counterparts. These three pink *guilloche* enamel eggs are surmounted by flowers set with rose cut diamonds and a half pearl. They are on a silver chain in the original box.

Another favorite was miniature paintings or portraits displayed in screens, each one a feat of perfection. The principle artists of these tiny masterpieces were Konstantin Krijitski, Johannes Zehngraf until his death in 1908, and then Vassily Zuieff. The workmaster who supervised the production of the egg generally had his initials inscribed on the bottom of the piece, alongside the Fabergé name. Of course, it was likely to have been one of his craftsmen who was responsible for the workmanship. From first plans to final product, the eggs would take at least 12 months, and possibly even years to create.

At first Fabergé produced eggs at the rate of one a year, which was given by the Czar to his wife. Following the death of Alexander III, and the accession of Nicholas II, the production rate was doubled so the Czar could present one to his wife and one to his widowed mother. Fabergé allowed his imagination to run riot, tackling subjects that most goldsmiths would dismiss as out of hand as impractical or plain impossible. Bainbridge enquired of Carl's son, Agathon Fabergé, the price of the eggs and was told they cost the Czars 30,000 roubles apiece. This is probably the price of the later, more exotic examples. Undoubtedly part of the charm of the Imperial eggs was the pleasure taken in creating them, and the joy both of giving, and receiving. Their express purpose was to inspire rapturous delight. It is important too to remember that Nicholas, especially, was devoted to his wife. The eggs he presented to her were not gifts inspired by duty or guilt but genuine love.

History has long accepted that 56 or 57 eggs were made by Fabergé for the Russian royals. The fate of every single one is not known although historical detectives and sleuths of the art world have done fine work in tracing 47 in a worldwide Easter egg hunt.

However, after studying the company records Russian art historian Valentin Skurlov announced that only 50 were crafted for the royals. The remainder he says were fakes or ones made for customers other than the Czars.

The final Imperial eggs, made in 1917, were never delivered to the royals. The Prime Minister, Alexander Kerensky, blocked the transaction. Still, we know the eggs were spartan in appearance and were afterwards decorated in an inappropriately luxuriant manner.

About a dozen eggs were made by Fabergé at the behest of other wealthy clients, among them the Pine Cone egg — made in 1900 with its "surprise" of an automated elephant — for Siberian gold mine owner Alexander Ferdinandovich Kelch. The exquisite gift was for his wife Barbara who was presented with six more Fabergé eggs by her industrialist husband. Kelch is thought to have been one of Fabergé's gold suppliers.

The couple, who married in 1894, lived at one of the most fashionable addresses in St Petersburg. However, despite their wealth, they were unable to find happiness together. They separated in 1904 and ultimately divorced. Kelch remained in Russia even after the revolution while his ex-wife fled to Paris where she sold most, if not all, of her prized eggs. He found work in the mining industry in Siberia where he married again. In 1924, he returned to St Petersburg — by now re-named Leningrad — and was jobless until he began selling cigarettes on the street. For a while he wrote to Barbara and she sent him money apparently hoping he would join her once more. In 1928, Kelch decided to abandon the idea of leaving Russia, opting to stay with his second family, and the letters between he and Barbara stopped. Two years after that, Kelch was arrested, tried and sentenced to hard labor.

Exotic Fabergé eggs were also created for Consuelo Vanderbilt, the Duchess of Marlborough; a silver wedding anniversary egg for Zenaida Yousupoff, a Russian royal, and the Ice Egg for Dr. Emmanuel Nobel (1859–1932), nephew of the Swedish inventor Alfred Nobel and oil company director.

These are less celebrated than the Imperial collection. Their very existence has also muddied the waters on the study of the Imperial eggs with various Kelch eggs being wrongly described as those made for the Czars.

**Above:** The Pine Cone egg, made for Barbara Kelch, was for many years mistaken as an Imperial egg. The workmaster in charge of making the jeweled *guilloche* enamel Easter egg was Michael Perchin in St Petersburg. Made of oxidized silver, the elephant bore ivory tusks and sat snugly in a molded compartment inside the egg. A testament to the skill of Fabergé craftsmen, the rider was an enameled figure, which sat on a gold fringed red and green saddle cloth. On each side there were three rose cut diamond decorations, one of which disguised a key hole. One of five automatons made by Faberge, the mechanism is likely to have been imported from France.

**Above:** The Pine Cone egg, (seen on page 35) with the elephant in its compartment.

**Above:** The Nobel Ice egg, made for Emmanuel Nobel, is white frosted enamel with a silver rim mounted with seed pearls. Inside, continuing the ice theme, lies a pendant with a tiny watch face. It is believed to have been made in 1910.

**Right:** One of the largest eggs made by Fabergé, this was presented to Barbara Kelch by her husband in 1901. It is carved from one piece of nephrite which was then set in a two-color gold cast fashion like a tree. The apple blossoms dotted over the cast have enamel petals and rose cut diamonds at the center, with gold leaves. The original case stamped with "Faberge" and bearing the Imperial warrant still exists.

Resurrection Egg
Date: 1887
Height: 3 7/8 inches
Marks: MP*, crossed anchors, 56

Sitting on a base embellished with pearls, rose diamonds and brilliant diamonds it is the single example of an Imperial egg bearing direct reference to the story of Easter. Inside a clear rock crystal egg, Christ is rising from the tomb, watched by two angels. The figures are constructed of enameled gold. There is no surprise within. The halves of the egg are held together with a line of rose diamonds and it suggests the style of the Italian Renaissance. The bidding for this egg reached £110 before it was sold at the Christie's auction on March 15, 1934.

Spring Flowers Egg
Date: 1890
Height: 3 1/2 inches
Marks: MP*, FABERGÉ, crossed anchors, 56

A fancy piece inspired by the era of France's Bourbon kings, the gold egg is enameled in red and encased in a golden cage. After releasing a diamond-set clasp the "surprise" is revealed — a rose diamond-studded platinum basket of spring flowers with garnet centers and gold stems, no bigger than 1 1/2 inches in height.

Azova Egg
Date: 1891
Length: 3 7/8 inches
Marks: MP*, crossed anchors, 72

On the outside, the egg lying horizontal and made from jasper (a variety of quartz), is heavy with gold and diamond scrolls. When a ruby clasp is opened a beautifully crafted model ship in gold, the *Pamiat Azova*, on which Nicholas as Czaraveitch embarked on a round-the-world voyage the previous year, is found nestling in waves of green velvet. Perchin was assisted by craftsman Yuri Nicolai.

## Caucasus Egg

Date: 1893

Height: 3 5/8 inches

Marks: MP*, crossed anchors, 72

Mimicking the style of Louise XV, the red enameled egg given by Alexander III to his wife is ornately decorated with wreaths and swags. On four sides there are pearl-edged doors which open to reveal views of Abastouman, the family's retreat in the Caucasus, painted by Krijitski. It was here that the couple's younger son George was virtually confined due to ill health. When the egg is held up to the light George's portrait can be seen through the smooth-faced diamond on its crown.

## Renaissance Egg

Date: 1894

Length: 5 1/4 inches

Marks: MP*. FABERGÉ, crossed anchors, 56

The final egg created for Alexander III lies horizontal on a gold base enameled with red and green flower motifs. It is made from a form of agate and the milky surface is covered with a trellis of white enamel gold bands with each intersection disguised by a diamond and ruby mini-buckle. On its top the year is picked out in diamonds. Although the egg opens its surprise is long since lost.

## Gold Pelican Egg

Date: 1897

Height: 4 1/8 inches

Marks: MP*, crossed anchors, 56

Another gold egg but this one lacks the enamel so familiar on Fabergé items. Its feature is an enameled and diamond-studded pelican — the emblem of motherhood — standing on top of the egg while the egg unfolds into an eight-panel screen of perfectly executed miniature paintings. The subjects of the pictures were institutions for the education of girls from noble families to which the Dowager Empress Marie lent her patronage.

## Coronation Egg

Date: 1897

Height: 5 inches

Marks: MP*, crossed anchors

Given by the Czar to his wife in the year following the coronation, the surface of the egg with its yellow enamel is reminiscent of the dress worn by the Czarina at this opulent event. Inside the surprise is a perfect replica of the coach which carried them there. Although less than four inches in length the coach has a painted ceiling and let-down steps. The name Wigström can be seen on the egg's inside surface. Owner of the egg today is the New York-based *Forbes* Magazine Collection.

Lilies of the Valley Egg

Date: 1898

Height: 5 5/16 inches (closed)

Marks: MP*, crossed anchors, 56

This exquisite Art Nouveau egg is gold with a rose-colored enamel surface standing upright on green-gold legs. Climbing up its sides are lily of the valley stems, each flower a pearl tipped with rose diamonds. When a pearl button on the side is turned a geared mechanism sends for three miniature portraits at the top of the egg, of Nicholas II and his two eldest daughters, Olga and Tatiana, painted by Zehngraf.

Madonna Lily Egg

Date: 1899

Height: 10 5/8 inches

Marks: MP* YL (the initials of Yakov Lyapunov, inspector of the St Petersburg Standards Board) 56

This upright egg given by the Czar to his wife is also a cleverly designed clock, with a static arrow pointer and a revolving dial, its numbers picked out in diamonds. It is topped with a bunch of madonna lilies, made from pale onyx, the pistils of which are three rose diamonds. The key to wind the clock is gold.

Pansy Egg

Date: 1899

Height: 5 3/4 inches

Marks: MP*

An Art Nouveau egg fashioned from nephrite and held in a twisted gilt silver frame decorated with enameled, gem-studded pansies. Inside there is a heart-shaped easel covered with 11 tiny enameled gold covers which spring open at the touch of a button to reveal miniature portraits of the Imperial family. It was given by the Czar to his wife.

## Trans-Siberian Railway Egg

Date: 1900

Height: 10 3/4 inches

Marks: MP*, YL, FABERGÉ, crossed anchors, 56

Construction on the Trans-Siberian Express running from Moscow to the distant port of Vladivostock on the Sea of Japan began in the 1880s under the orders of Alexander III who understood the military advantages such a line would give. When this egg was made the railway line was incomplete. The 5,578 miles (9,297 km) of track which form today's line were not finally laid until 1914. However, the extraordinary feat of engineering which allowed the line to plough through some of Russia's most inhospitable territory was clearly evident at the turn of the century.

The egg is gold, coated with green enamel and decorated. Around its center runs a broad silver band on which a map of the railway is engraved. Each station is represented by a precious stone. Atop the egg is a three-headed eagle in gold bearing the Imperial Crown. Supporting it are three griffins with swords and shields. These mythical birds, symbols of the Russian royals, squat on a white onyx base.

Inside the egg is a miniature of the express train and four carriages that traveled on the route fashioned in gold and platinum. Further, the engine is clockwork and can be wound up with a key to pull its five replica coaches, altogether measuring almost 16 inches. The last of the coaches is designed to be a traveling church while others are marked: Smoking, Non-Smoking and Ladies Only.

## Cuckoo Egg

Date: 1900

Height: 8 1/8 inches

Marks: MP*

The front of the egg bears a clock face set in red gold and surrounded by pearls. This upright egg is held secure between three white enameled pillars emerging from an ornate base. Far more remarkable is its "surprise." When a button is pushed on the back of the clock, a gold grille on the egg top lifts and out comes a feathered cuckoo with ruby eyes standing on gold legs, flapping its wings and singing. When its song is done it descends back into the egg.

## Peter The Great Egg

Date: 1903

Height: 4 inches

Marks: MP*, crossed anchors, 56

Marking the bi-centennial of St Petersburg — the city founded by Peter the Great as his "window on the empire" — here was an extravagant egg of gold inlaid with diamonds and rubies. The top flips open to reveal the "surprise," a model replica of the statue of Peter The Great in Neva, that mechanically rises from the depths of the egg. The model, made of gold, rests on a base of sapphire.

Uspensky Cathedral Egg

Date: 1904

Height: 14 1/2 inches

Marks: FABERGÉ 1904

A faithful reproduction of the Uspensky Cathedral where the Russian Czars were crowned. The egg perches on cathedral towers, and peering through its windows, one can see the cathedral interior. The mechanics of the piece allow its tiny clocks to chime and play a traditional hymn.

Peacock Egg

Date: 1908

Height: 6 inches

Marks: HW

A delightfully exquisite piece, the egg itself is breathtaking. It is made of rock crystal and is snug on a rococo stand. However, inside perched in a golden tree is the real star, a peacock which can be lifted from the branches and wound up to walk, move its head and even fan its impressive tail. Craftsman Dorofeev, who spent three years making the bird, was later singled out for special praise by Eugene Fabergé for his patience and skill.

Romanov Tercentenary Egg

Date: 1913

Height: 7 5/16 inches

Marks: HW, FABERGÉ, 1913, 72

The royal dynasty began in 1613 with the rule of Michael Romanov, ending a period of turbulence in the country's history known as the "Time of Troubles." To mark the anniversary, Fabergé came up with what is considered his most elaborate egg. Across the surface of the white-enameled gold egg are 18 portraits on ivory, in diamond frames, of the most notable Czars. Inside lies a blue steel globe, one side reflecting the Russian Empire in 1613, and the other in 1913. In the wake of the Tercentenary the "old Russian Style" became fashionable once more. The permanent home of the Tercentenary egg is the State Museum in Moscow.

Red Cross Egg

| | |
|---|---|
| Date: | 1915 |
| Height: | 3 1/8 inches |
| Marks: | Unknown |

This gift to the Czar's mother now seems a moving emblem of the devastating European conflict and ever-impending doom. Lacking the usual clutch of stones, the egg is white enamel on silver, featuring two red crosses and the words (in Russian): "Greater love hath no man than this, that a man lay down his life for his friends." Inside there was a screen of miniatures showing the Czarina and her four daughters in the uniforms of the red cross. The Dowager Empress was the head of the Russian Red Cross during the First World War. The Czarina and her two eldest daughters, the Grand Duchesses Olga and Tatiana, donned the uniforms to nurse wounded soldiers in the hospital at Tsarkoe Selo.

Steel Military Egg

| | |
|---|---|
| Date: | 1916 |
| Height: | 4 inches |
| Marks: | HW, FABERGÉ, 72 |

Given the privations that Russia was suffering during the First World War, Fabergé knew the egg should reflect a measure of austerity. As a result it was made of blackened steel and stood on pillars depicting artillery shells. Within the egg is an easel with a miniature of Czar Nicholas and his son conferring with generals at the front. The Czar was away at the front that Easter. The egg was presented to the Czarina by Carl Fabergé's son Eugene.

STONE CARVINGS

Birds, elephants, kangaroos, dogs, fish, rabbits, horses, frogs, pigs, snakes, snails, cats, rats, mice, chimps, bears and hippos were all immortalized by Fabergé. There was room in his menagerie even for the more unlikely beasts — the aardvark, the warthog and the duck-billed platypus.

The inspiration for Fabergé for the genre was the Japanese *netsuke*, small cord-weights which feature in that country's national dress. *Netsuke* probably originated in the 14th century. Although finely carved the *netsuke* were smooth so they did not catch on clothing. Western dress was introduced to Japan in the late 18th century but, far from spelling the end for *netsuke*, it assured them of a future as they were exported to Europe and America where they were sought after for their ornamental value.

At first *netsuke* were made of wood but later materials including ivory, amber, jade and coral were used by makers. Apart from animals *netsuke* carvers depicted gods and demons.

One of Fabergé's most celebrated commissions was to re-create some of the farm animals at Sandringham as a gift to be given by Edward VII to his wife Queen Alexandra on her birthday, December 1. The suggestion came from Alice Keppel.

It can be hard to discern genuine Fabergé from copies for few were marked. And an animal bearing the name Fabergé may not be genuine as the forger issued the hallmark with ease. Yet the aficionado will look for a lively caricature oozing charm, qualities which so many copies singularly fail to replicate.

**Top**: Jasper elephant with rose diamond eyes, its trunk turned towards its mouth.

**Above**: A gem set silver vodka cup in the form of an elephant, with *cabochon* ruby eyes. Markings, which identify it as the produce of Michael Perchin in St Petersburg and the inventory number are visible beneath the tail.

**Top**: Made of rhodonite, this model made in St Petersburg in about 1890 measures just a little over an inch in length. It was once the property of the wife of the procurator general of St Petersburg.

**Above**: Kalgan jasper elephant with rose diamond eyes.

49

**Left**: Thought to have once belonged to the Empress Marie, "Percy" is a bowenite elephant bearing an enameled howdah on its back standing some nine inches in height. From the workmaster Michael Perchin in about 1890.

**Above left:** This stylized figure of an owl, made of jasper with gold mounted tourmaline eyes, standing little more than three inches high, was once the property of Princess Victoria, daughter of King Edward VII.

**Above right:** A carved bloodstone mouse with gold mounted, rose cut diamond eyes made in the Fabergé workshops in about 1890.

**Above**: Humorous caricature of an elephant in the style of Fabergé made out of nephrite, its wide face set alight with *cabochon* ruby eyes.

**Above**: Dalmatian dog carved in
the Fabergé workshop in about
1890 from Russian moss agate to
simulate the markings.

**Above**: An endearing baby cormorant carved from Russian bowenite with rubies for eyes. Made in about 1890.

**Above, left to right**: Carved from agate, this realistic model of a chicken has gold legs and rose cut diamond eyes and stands two and a half inches high. The squatting ostrich linked to Henrik Wigström has gold legs tucked beneath and green stone eyes. A cockerel with gold legs and rose-cut diamond eyes made out of agate in the Fabergé workshops is three inches in height.

**Left, left to right:** Realistically carved in bowenite this model frog has gold-mounted ruby eyes in a fitted case stamped with the name of London jeweler's Wartski. An American bison carved from bowenite, with gold mounted ruby eyes; was auctioned with its box stamped "A la Vieille Russie," New York. Rose cut diamond eyes light up the face of this bowenite rhinoceros which comes in a fitted case stamped Wartski, London.

**Below left, left to right:** Carved quartz model of a chick with red stone eyes measuring half an inch in length. A humorously carved elephant with red stone eyes measuring an inch in length. Marble model of an owl with moonstone eyes, one and a quarter inches high. Carved from bowenite, this pig in humorous style comes in a fitted case stamped Wartski, London.

**Above**: Carved from agate, a realistic model of a kitten
(left) with red stone eyes. Upright rabbit (right) in
carved from marble in humorous style.

**Above:** This carved duck is made from different colored hardstones and has diamond set eyes.

CIGARETTE CASES

FABERGÉ

FABERGÉ cigarette cases were the epitome of style for the nicotine-addicted masses of the early 20th century. Some — like the silver case in sunrise pattern with a *cabochon* sapphite thumb piece, made for the Grand Duke Michael Michaelovitch and delivered in January 1914 — were very elegant. Others revealed humor, like the case with a miniature painting of a loving couple being spied upon by two peasant women. The Russian royals often gave them as gifts. Czar Nicholas II presented one of his generals with a case made of enameled gold and diamond studded with a rose diamond frame surrounding a miniature portrait of the giver. Gentlemen of the day considered it necessary to own three or four. Characteristically they measured about four inches in length, longer if they included a compartment for matches.

One of the most romantic stories linked to the Fabergé industry centers on cigarette cases and came to light late in the 20th century. An elderly Frenchman by the name of Charles Antoine Roger Luzarche d'Azay bequeathed a collection of cigarette cases to the Musée des Arts Decoratifs in Paris in the early 1960s. Eighteen of the cases were made in the Fabergé workshops between 1901 and 1915. D'Azay was once in the French secret service but little else was known of his life.

The cases were wrought with symbolism, entwined serpents, crescent moons and so forth, pointing to a love affair. There were also cases which listed French military campaigns, and there was one etched with a map of the Nile Valley with eight places marked in gem-stones. One case even had a secret compartment containing the portrait of a woman. The mystery of the cases remained intact until 1993 when friends of d'Azay finally revealed that he had been in love but his mistress, Princess Cécile Murat was married. Scholars deduced that she had presented her lover with the cases but many questions are still unanswered. The most intriguing, perhaps is the significance of the stones on the Nile case. Were they indicative of espionage activities carried out by the spy? Or were they venues for secret trysts between the illicit pair? Investigation continues but the facts are likely to remain veiled by the passage of time.

The largest collection of Fabergé cigarette boxes belong to American investor, author and fine arts expert John Traina, who lives in San Francisco. Traina, former husband of novelist Danielle Steele, has written a book *The Fabergé Case* on the distinctive beauty of the cigarette boxes.

**Above:** The cigarette case lid depicts a map of the roads leading to Livadia, a favorite venue of the Russian royals lying about three miles south west of Yalta. It was on the luxurious estate at Livadia that Alexander III died. Following the revolution, it was converted to a workers' sanitarium.

**Above left**: Yellow metal cigarette box made in the workshops of Gabriel Niukkanen in St Petersburg for Fabergé.

**Above right**: Jeweled yellow mounted silver gilt cigarette case from the workmaster Anders Nevalainen in St Petersburg.

**Below left**: Moscow-made white metal cigarette case with a Mumm Cordon Vert champagne bottle.

**Below right**: Diamond and opaque enamel cigarette case, the enamel band encrusted with rose cut diamonds. Marked as a Fabergé item out of Moscow.

**Above**: Jeweled, gold mounted nephrite cigarette case made by Michael Perchin in about 1890.

**Left**: Elegantly designed cigarette cases were Fabergé's speciality. This oblong example made under workmaster Henrik Wigström has a *guilloche* enamel on its gold body, a thumbpiece with rose diamond setting and foiled chalcedony panels at either end. Wigstrom chose a brilliant diamond above rose diamonds for the thumbpiece.

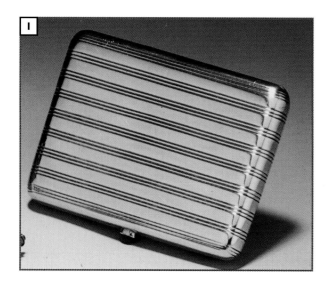

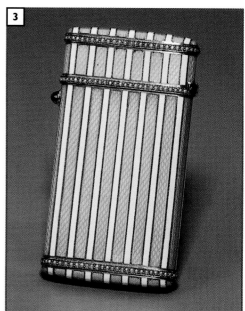

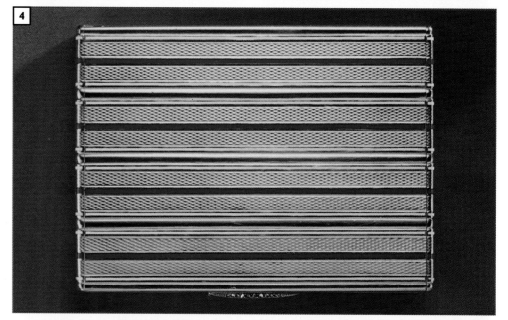

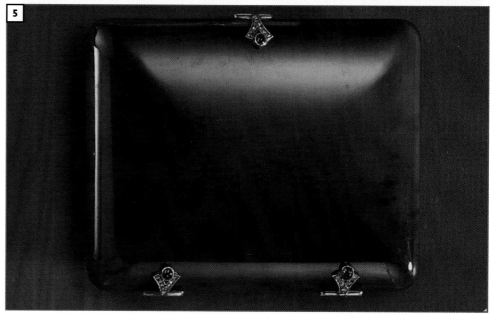

**1**: A silver cigarette case with an elegant ribbon design bearing the mark of Fabergé, the Imperial warrant and the inventory number 30875.

**2**: Striped with opaque enamel and gilt decoration, this cigarette case opens at the push of an oval, cushion cut diamond.

**3**: Stripes of translucent yellow enamel and opaque white are dissected by three bands of split pearls on this cigarette case. The pushpiece is a *cabochon* ruby.

**4**: A jeweled, gold and enamel case decorated overall with gold engine-turned bands between narrow blue and white enamel stripes.

**5**: A jeweled, gold and nephrite case, the hinges and claspe are set with rose-cut diamonds and *cabochon* rubies.

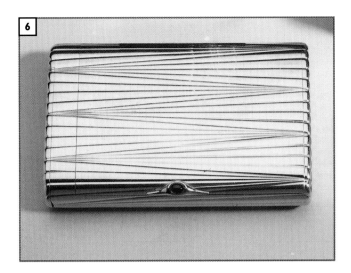

6: Gold cigarette case, with gold-mounted sapphire thumbpiece.

7: Jeweled gold and parcel-gilt *guilloche* case with a rose cut diamond encrusted Imperial Russian double-headed eagle.

**Below left:** A Russian Imperial double-headed eagle set with a diamond illuminates the corner of this gold cigarette case. It is inscribed inside the cover with the words, "Given by the Grand Duke Michael of Russia (Czarevich) to Lord Suffield, Feb 1901."

**Below center top:** Made in St Petersburg in the workshop of Karl Lundell this cigarette case has a *cabochon* sapphire thumbpiece in a fitted case stamped "Wartski, London."

**Below center bottom:** A cigarillo case with the initials "VC" engraved inside. Markings indicate it was made in Moscow and exported to London in 1907.

**Below right:** A jeweled two-color gold match case.

# JEWELRY

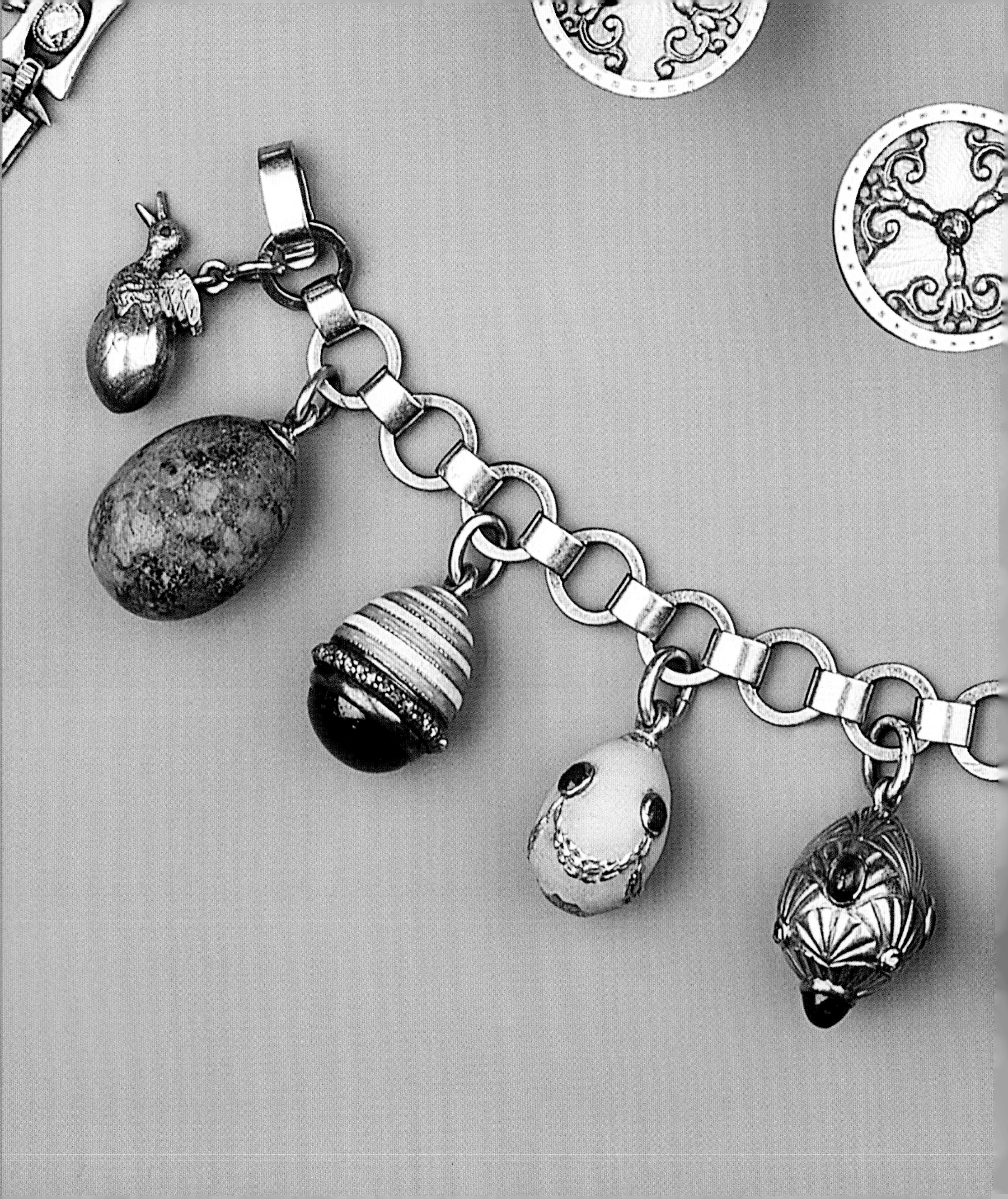

The items of jewelry or accessories known as *bijouterie* attract the least attention in the array of Fabergé goods. There's comparatively little of it left. The monied classes in late 19th century Russia were singularly unimpressed by glittering diamonds and sparkling sapphires and so did not value them highly. Sometimes they were traded. At any rate, they certainly were not considered collectable.

Following the revolution such items were used to stimulate revenue for the government. They were either sold to foreign buyers or melted down — as was much of the Fabergé silverware.

**Above:** A portrait by Zehngraf of Grand Duchess Elizabeth Feodorovna, sister of of the Empress Alexandra who was widowed when her husband Grand Duke Sergei Alexandrovich was assassinated in Moscow in the 1905 uprising. Afterward she became a nun and devoted herself to charitable works until she was arrested following the revolution, deported to Siberia and murdered in a mineshaft. She was canonized by the Russian Orthodox Church in 1995.

**Right:** A selection of small pieces used as pendants.

**Opposite page:** *Peridot* and diamond necklace, bracelet and earrings by the workmaster August Holmstrom in St Petersburg. The pendant on the necklace is missing.

68

**Right:** The initials of Carl Fabergé authenticate this pendant which has swirling foliage around a central ruby, made in Moscow.

**Opposite page, top left inset:** Oval amythest and diamond brooch made in St Petersburg for Faberge in about 1890.

**Opposite page top right inset:** Jeweled oyster *guilloche* enamel cuff links from the workshops of Henrik Wigström.

**Opposite page above:** This bracelet features 11 jeweled, enamel and hardstone miniature Easter eggs.

**Opposite page center:** Eight *cabochon* sapphires linked by yellow metal and set with diamonds to form a bracelet.

**Opposite page below:** A jeweled brooch made by workmaster August Hollming in St Petersburg and given by Czar Nicholas II to the daughter of the artist Franz Roubaud, famous as a painter of battle scenes.

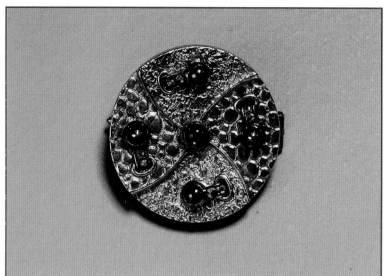

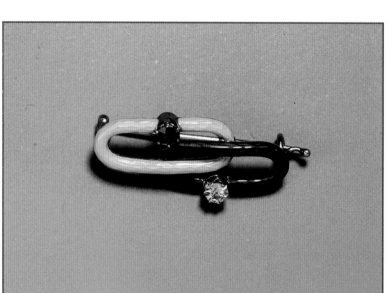

72

**Top left**: A circular brooch just over an inch in diameter decorated with rose cut diamond and *cabochon* ruby motifs, with a *cabochon* sapphire at its center.

**Above left**: Two interlocking oval bands form this brooch, one in red *guilloche* enamel bearing a diamond, the other in white *guilloche* enamel set with a ruby.

**Above right**: One of nine brooches of the same design produced by Fabergé workshops in St Petersburg to mark the Romanov tercentenary in 1913. Workmaster Erik Kollin is credited with this Imperial Russian double-headed eagle set with rose-cut diamonds.

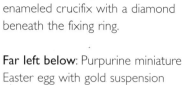

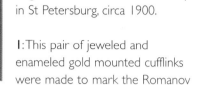

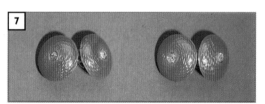

**Far left**: Jeweled gold and enameled crucifix with a diamond beneath the fixing ring.

**Far left below**: Purpurine miniature Easter egg with gold suspension ring from Victor Aarne's workshop in St Petersburg, circa 1900.

**1**: This pair of jeweled and enameled gold mounted cufflinks were made to mark the Romanov tercentenary in 1913.

**2**: Pink moss agate cufflinks held within a silver-mounted rose-cut diamond rim.

**3**: Lozenge-shaped cufflinks with four diamonds in the middle emanating from sunburst *guilloche* ground enamel.

**4**: Jeweled, emerald cufflinks from workmaster August Hollming.

**5**: Jeweled, *guilloche* enamel gold-mounted cufflinks.

**6**: Jeweled, *guilloche* enamel gold mounted cufflinks.

**7**: Erik Kollin is the workmaster behind these circular cufflinks made before 1908.

**8**: Jeweled, *guilloche* enamel, gold mounted cufflinks made for Grand Duke Cyril Vladimirovich.

**9**: These diamond-decked cufflinks come in their original purple presentation case.

73

**Previous pages:** An owl-shaped bell push. See page 85

**Below:** Under two inches in height this parasol handle nevertheless boasts a *guilloche* enamel finish with a gold and seed pearl border. It is from the workmaster Michael Perchin.

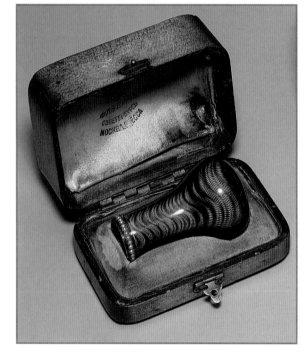

FABERGÉ

**FABERGÉ's work typified the Edwardian era when extraordinary detail was invested in the most day-to-day objects. Take, for example, the humble bell push.**

The end of the 19th century brought with it the advent of electricity and, in its wake, the bell pushes which would soon adorn the most stylish residences across Europe. Fabergé was presented with a new opportunity in design, his only constraint being the necessities of house wiring and workings. Evidently he reveled in the challenge.

For customers in England came a bell push in the form of a five-inch wide silver crab with a blue chalcedony shell, each protruding moonstone eye serving as an operating button.

Other bell pushes came as panels which were ornately decorated with silver gilt flourishes and finished with a button made of a semi-precious stone.

Russian gentry and their English and French counterparts also had Fabergé at their fingertips when they took up their canes or parasols. From the Fabergé workshops came a range of handles, many in his favorite enamel finishes and featuring gold, silver and gemstone finishing touches. The most self-indulgent of the era even sought to have riding crops with Fabergé handles.

This was another area which the design guru would make his own. His fans were richly embelished fashion statements, as those that have survived can prove. It was the guard stick behind which the fan could close which bore the Fabergé hallmarks.

He might choose to have them enameled, like so many of his finest objects. Yet some were gold and studded with gemstones and others adorned with tortoiseshell.

Consider the Fabergé fan now residing in the Kremlin — a five-inch gold guard stick decorated with scrollwork, crystals and diamonds, the fan sticks made of Mother of Pearl inlaid with gold. The scene depicted when the fan was spread was one of soldiers courting ladies in a park, painted by Van Garden, one of the top fan-decorators of his generation and enlivened with sequins.

Czar Nicholas II presented a bejeweled fan to Princess Victoria, second daughter of Edward VII and Queen Alexandra, as she cruised the Mediterranean on the yacht *Standart*, belonging to the Russian royals.

Two fans are kept in the *Forbes* magazine collection. One has a rock crystal handle, with enamel and diamonds, and white ostrich feathers at its center. It is thought to have belonged to the Grand Duchess Xena, sister of Czar Nicholas and was sported by her at a costume ball held in the Winter Palace in St Petersburg in 1903. Even as long ago 1908 it changed hands for £90.

The second *Forbes* collection fan has a similarly enameled and diamond-crusted guard stick but this time the inner leaf is made of exquisite gold gauze interspersed with miniatures.

Fans were vital accessories at imperial weddings. Grand Duchess Olga Alexandrovna received a Fabergé fan from Czar Nicholas when she married Prince Peter of Oldenburg on July 27, 1901.

The guard stick was, once again, gold overlaid this time with yellow enamel and rich with diamonds. It also bore the monogram of the Duchess. The fan leaf shows the Duchess and her intended taking part in Russian marriage customs alongside a view of the Oldenburg Palace in St Petersburg.

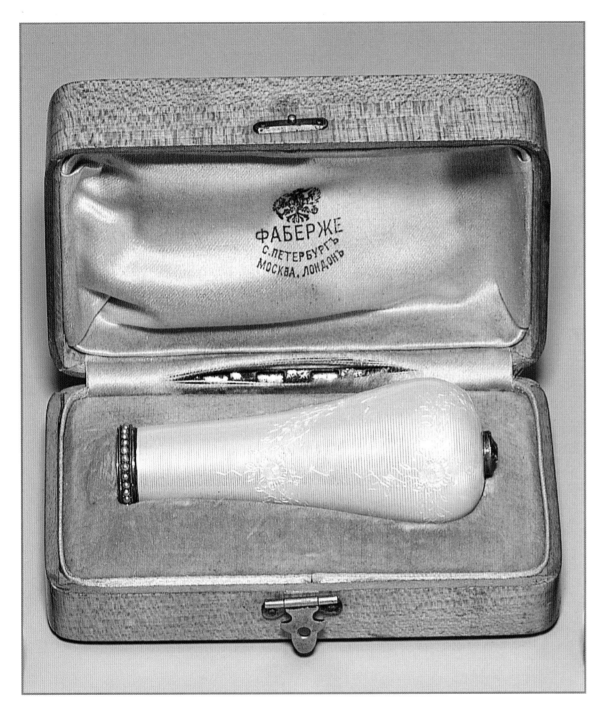

**Above:** Two-color gold mounted *guilloche* enamel parasol handle made in the workshops of Henrik Wigström.

**Above left:** Parasol handle of *guilloche* enamel with bulbous body in translucent white. There is a seed pearl border and pale green finial. Although the item is unmarked its box bears the Fabergé stamp.

FAB

**Above**: A bell push made in the form of a pear, with a chased gold stem on one side and a *cabochon* garnet push piece on the other. This piece was auctioned with its original fitted case bearing the words "Fabergé St Petersburg, Moscow, Odessa."

**Left**: A cane handle made of quartzite and decorated with silver gilt beading emerging from sapphire set rosettes. On the top lies a tigress carved in agate.

**Right:** This rock crystal parasol handle has, encased inside, a hardstone bulldog puppy complete with collar and seed-pearl bell around its neck.

**Left**: Silver mounted palisander bell push from workmaster Victor Aarne in St Petersburg.

**Below**: A paper knife with its handle decorated with *cloisonné* enamel and set with gems.

**Bottom left**: A silver gilt *guilloche* enamel bell push with a *cabochon* moonstone push piece.

**Bottom right**: From the collection of Grand Duchess Olga Alexandrovna, daughter of Czar Alexander III, comes this jeweled and *cloisonné* enameled parasol handle out of the workshop of Michael Perchin.

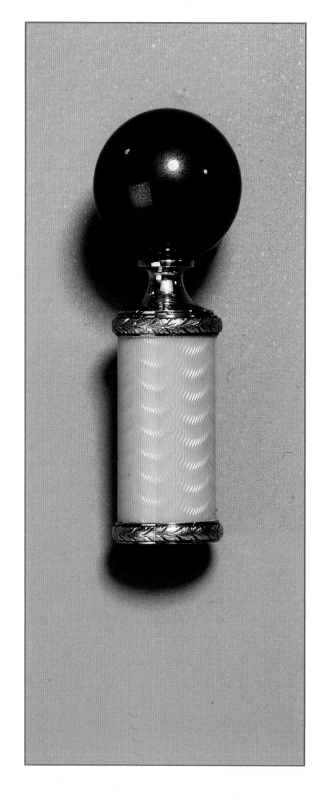

**Above:** A *guilloche* enamel and nephrite cane handle with a hardstone sphere on its end.

**Above**: A bell push in the semblance of an owl, the eyes set into a nephrite base which was fitted for electricity. Made under the workmaster Julius Rappoport in St Petersburg.

# THERE WERE NO BOUNDARIES

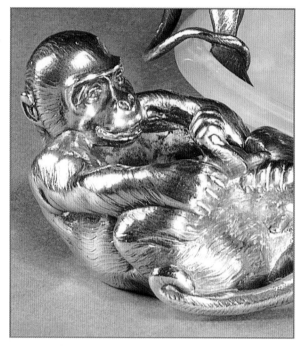

**THERE WERE NO BOUNDARIES** in Fabergé's vision. Consequently the range of his work was immense. His most famous or familiar have been treated in separate chapters, yet there was much, much more in his repertoire.

The best dressed dinner tables had the mark of Fabergé upon them. His workshops produced exquisitely designed tableware — dinner services and tea sets — as well as glasses and serving bowls. When it came to salt and pepper holders his imagination ran riot, and thus there appeared a tabletop "bidet" of Louis XVI cabriolet style, the ornate lid protecting a chamber pot full of salt. Cutlery, serviette rings, jugs, tureens and serving ladles were all made with patience, skill and originality, for style-conscious hosts.

In the study, Fabergé also found his niche. There were envelope knives with richly decorated handles, pens, pencil-holders and handseals which reflect an era when great importance was heaped upon handwritten correspondence, both personal and business. Nearby would rest a photograph of a fondly-held memory in a Fabergé frame. The time of day could be discerned from a distinctively Fabergé clock on the mantle.

Some Fabergé items romantically reflect high society a century ago, and its penchants. A profusion of snuff boxes were made with the Fabergé stamp. Snuff boxes, like larger multi-purpose boxes, bore a vast range of designs — square, rectangular, oval or circular — some were enameled, some made from silver, gold, nephrite, agate or other materials, including gun-metal. The array remains magnificent.

Further symbols of the time include lorgnettes, opera glasses and playing card cases.

**Previous pages:** A Fabergé vase. See page 106.

**Left and opposite page left:** Silver ashtray in the form of a monkey from the workshops of Julius Rappoport in St Petersburg measuring just over three inches in length.

**Opposite page center:** Oval bowenite bowl with two carved and chased monkeys as handles.

**Opposite page right:** Silver glue pot modeled humorously as an elephant.

**Right:** Pair of silver mounted nephrite candelabra made in the workshops of Julius Rappoport in about 1890.

**Right:** A set of two perfume flasks and a powder jar follow a similar theme, with glass cut in the shape of thistles and dandelions. The top is mauve *guilloche* enamel the neck is oyster enamel with rose diamonds and red gold scallops. The finials on the lid tops are pearl.

**Above**: Gold *guilloche* enamel and
gemset pillbox marked Fabergé
and traced back to the
workmaster Michael Perchin in
about 1880.

93

**Above**: Gold enamel and gemset snuffbox by Michael Perchin in about 1880. The central enamel plaque is believed to have been the work of Charles Jacques de Mailly (1740–1817).

**Above**: Workmaster Anders Nevalainen of St Petersburg is credited with this silver mounted *guilloche* enamel frame.

**Above**: Gilt and *guilloche* enamel wooden frame from the workmaster Anders Nevalainen in St Petersburg.

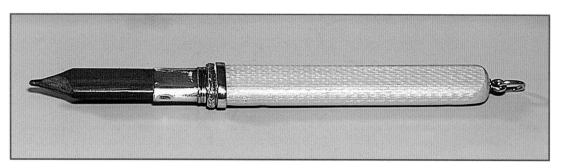

**Top**: Two-color gold and enamel taper stick marked under the base with the initials of Feodor Afanasev, a workmaster in St Petersburg between 1908 and 1917.

**Above**: Gold and *guilloche* enamel pencil holder.

**Right**: Gold mounted *guilloche* enameled pencil.

**Above**: Caviar spoon with a smoky quartz bowl and reeded stem leading to a rock crystal finial.

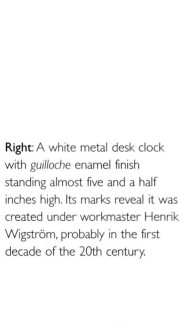

**Right**: A white metal desk clock with *guilloche* enamel finish standing almost five and a half inches high. Its marks reveal it was created under workmaster Henrik Wigström, probably in the first decade of the 20th century.

99

**Above**: A round silver gilt cake basket, the fluted body set on a raised foot. At its center lies à silver coin bearing the head of the Empress Marie.

**Above:** A traditional *kovsh* with a
lacquered red body. It was made
in Moscow but the workmaster
initials remain indistinct.

101

**Left**: A white metal perfume burner made by Fabergé's Moscow workmaster Konstantin Wakewa between 1899 and 1908. The border of the domed cover is engraved with the crowned interlaced initials of "RR."

**Above**: Made in the style of the
French King Louis XV, this silver
*jardiniere* is oval and perches on
four *rocaille* feet. It was made by
Fabergé's Moscow workshops
between 1880 and 1893.

**Above:** This scent flask has a hinged cover disguised by its gold texture to appear like jute cloth, tied with a twisted rope set with a brilliant diamond and *cabochon* sapphire. It stand just two and a half inches high.

**Above**: A table box standing three and a half inches high with rounded corners and gold cagework. Made in St Petersburg in about 1890, it has the inventory number 49168.

**Above:** This nephrite *kovsh* has the Imperial eagle set with rubies and rose diamonds on its flat handle.

**Right**: A crackle-glazed art
pottery vase with motifs of the
Pan-Slavic style.

**Above**: More Pan-Slavic designs embellish the lower body of this silver punch bowl made in 1912. It is engraved in Russian with the words "To Osip Ilych Safir from the Board of the Bessarabia-Tavrichesk Land Bank." The ladle is engraved "XXV," indicating that it was probably a long-service award.

**Above**: Michael Perchin oversaw
the making of this two-colored
gold mounted bowenite picture
frame. It was made in St
Petersburg around 1890.

**Above left**: A six-pointed star in red *guilloche* enamel surrounding a white enamel dial and gold hands pointing to arabic numbers. The clock was once the property of a Russian Grand Duke.

**Left**: A gold mounted enamel frame with a border of seed pearls surrounding the picture.

**Above**: Given as a gift by
Emmanuel Nobel, this is a six-sided
rock crystal plaque embellished
with mounted rose diamonds in
the pattern of snowflakes.

**Above**: A gold, silver gilt and enamel table thermometer still held in its original velvet and silk-lined wooden presentation box.

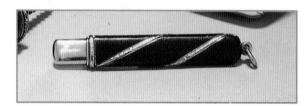

**Top**: A jeweled gold nephrite card case.

**Above**: An enameled gold pencil holder with the unrecorded workmaster's initials "AR."

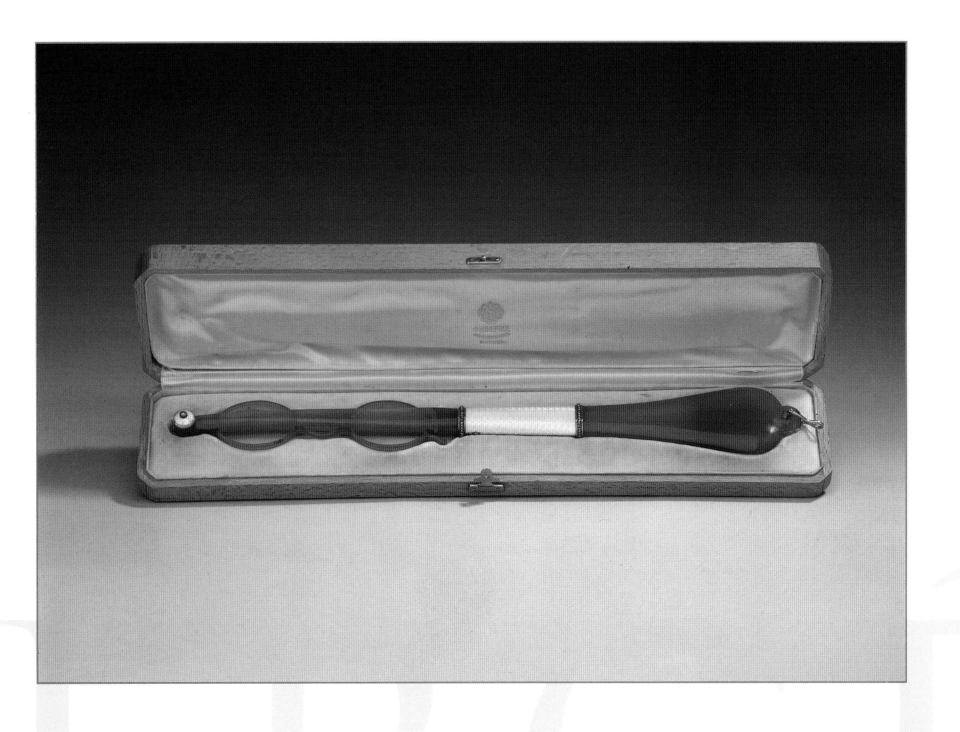

**Above:** The lavishness of this lorgnette made around 1900 sums up the art of Fabergé. It is made of gold, *guilloche* enamel and tortoiseshell set with diamonds.

**Above:** This four-footed oval silver tureen, a striking 16 and a half inches in length, was made in Moscow in about 1898 and bears the inventory number 12183.

TABI

**Above left**: Two-color gold nephrite dish in Fabergé style.

**Left**: A salt cellar in silver gilt with *cloisonné* enamel in the Pan-Slavic style.

EWARE

**Above, left to right:** A silver mounted palisander bowl made in Moscow; a glazed pottery bowl with silver ribbon bearing, once again, the unknown workmaster's initials "AR." Standing on four ball feet this silver vodka cup has a handle set with a silver ten *kopeck* coin dated 1799.

**Above**: With its handles decorated by cornucopia, swans and laurel wreaths this cutlery set is incomplete, lacking at least one dessert fork and eight table knives.

**Above**: A silver salt-shaker made in
Moscow in the form of a
floundering perch, its gasping
mouth pierced as the outlet.

RELIGIOUS PIECES

**Above:** This rare devotional frame made around 1890 in the Fabergé workshops under the guidance of Michael Perchin has, at its center, a rendition of the Lord's Prayer.

**Above**: An icon of St Nicholas with rays of enamel fanning out behind the brightly painted figure of the saint. The discs left and right of him contain images of Christ and the Virgin Mary.

**Above:** A christening set like this owes more to old England that to Russian Orthodoxy. Nevertheless, this is a Fabergé piece standing less than three inches high bearing the monogram "AAD."

# CUSTOMERS

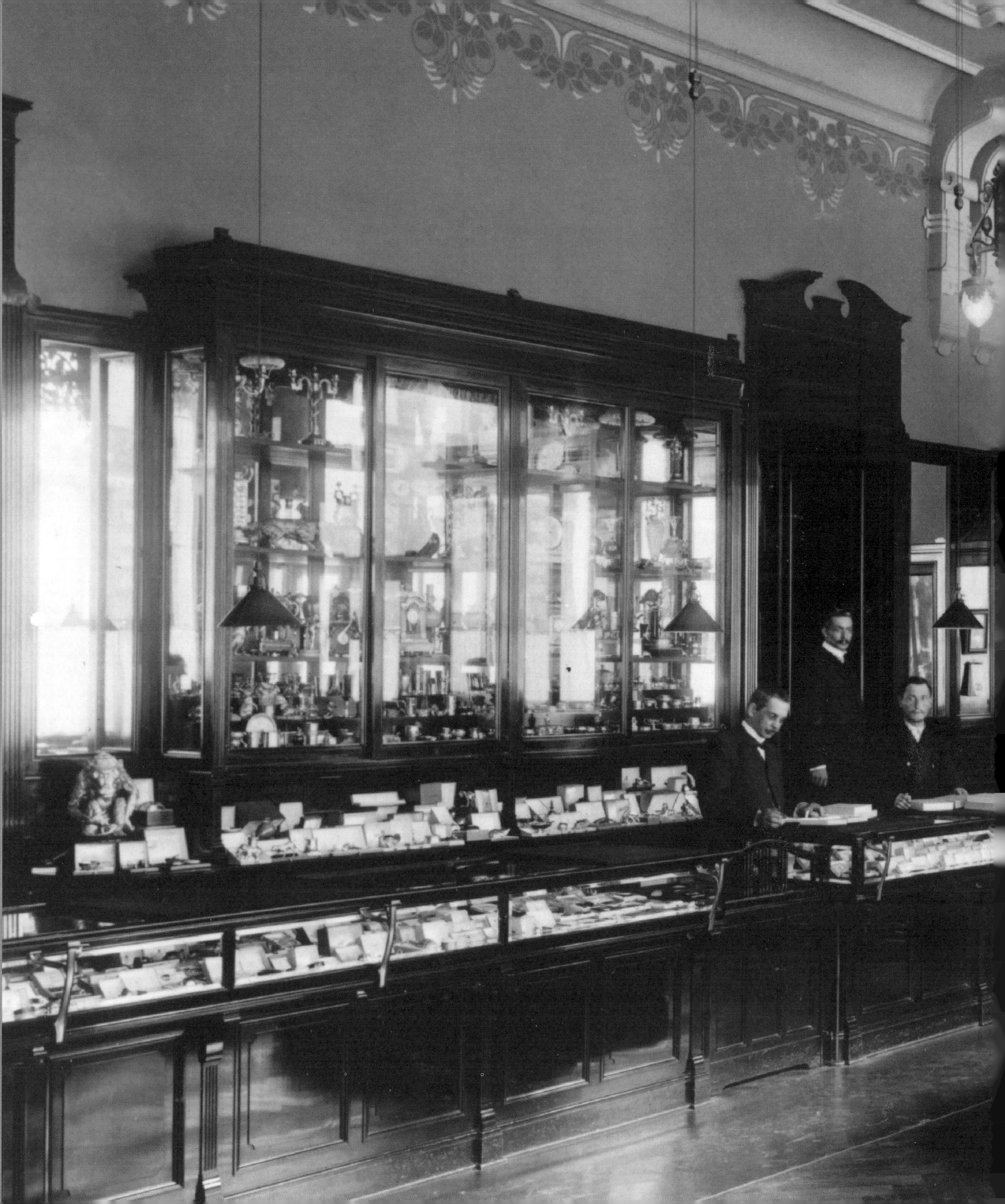

THE PRINCIPLE CLIENTS OF FABERGÉ

124

**Previous page**: Glass cases lined the Fabergé showrooms in St Petersburg amply displaying the artifacts.

**Above**: The Fabergé shopfront

**THE PRINCIPLE CLIENTS OF FABERGÉ were the Russian Czars Alexander III and Nicholas II. With patrons as influential as these no Russian craftsman needed to fear for the buoyancy of his business. A more consuming problem was how to remain in the good books of the Czars who might be offended by ill-thought-out concepts or clumsy design. Fabergé had sufficient amounts of charm, skill and foresight to maintain the grace and favor of the Russian royals.**

Alexander (1845–94) was a conservative, and arrogant army officer, more interested in the persecution of radicals and extending the powers of the police than in pursuing a social agenda which might have benefited the majority of his subjects. Alexander — a burly bear of a man — was passionately patriotic and anti-German in outlook. At a dinner party he once knotted a silver fork and threw it at the Austrian ambassador in a fury. When the train on which he was traveling with his family was de-railed by revolutionaries he saved their lives by holding up the roof of the dining car. Queen Victoria described him as "a sovereign whom I cannot look upon as a gentleman."

He was the son of the reformer Alexander II (1818–81), who was best remembered for emancipating the serfs and re-organizing the government of his rambling Russian empire.

It seems strange that a hardline son should be born of such a liberal. But Alexander III was a witness when his well-intentioned father was blown up by a bomb, hurled into his coach by a revolutionary. Although he lost a leg, an eye, and suffered other terrible injuries, it took the Czar 45 minutes to die. This agony clearly influenced the views of Alexander III who resorted to repression.

He married Princess Marie Dagmar of Denmark, sister of Queen Alexandra of England, who for years was haunted by the dreadful scenes of her father-in-law's assassination. The *raison d'etre* for the first Imperial egg is thought to have been to alieviate the Czarina's melancholy. It was Marie who propelled Fabergé to fame, believing him to be "a great, incomparable genius."

In 1891, Fabergé made an outstanding clock to mark the couple's silver wedding anniversary. Around a green onyx, diamond studded face fly 25 cast and chased cherubs bearing the attributes of Love and Music. Above the dial perches the Russian Imperial double-headed eagle. Like most clocks produced by Fabergé the internal mechanism was imported from the recognized international experts, the Swiss. It was bought for 18,585 roubles by 32 members of the extended Imperial family, when the average monthly salary for city dwellers in Russia was in the region of 33 roubles. In 1894, Czar Alexander died of kidney failure, brought about by an accident and years of hard drinking.

Meanwhile, Nicholas (1868–1918) was more in his grandfather's mold. Yet even if his natural inclination veered towards improving the lot of his subjects he was enticed into absolutism. Nicholas was notoriously weak and became fodder for unscrupulous ministers and other advisors. He was devoted to his wife, the German Princess Alix of Hesse-Damstadt who became known as the Czarina Alexandra.

Like her mother-in-law, she was beguiled by the work of Fabergé. Her favorite piece is acknowledged to be the Lilies of the Valley Basket, made for her in 1896. The numerous blooms are made of pearls which hang from nine gold stems

**Left**: Gold and *guilloche* enamel gemset cigarette case brought from Fabergé by Baron Maurice de Rothschild in 1913 and presented as a gift.

FROM

BARON MAURICE DE ROTHSCHILD

1913.

126

**Above**: An inside view of the cigarette case seen on the previous page engraved with the giver's name.

adorned with nephrite leaves held in a bed of spun green gold and platinum, looking for all the world like a mossy cushion. The fetching piece is in a wire basket, beneath which the following inscription appears (English translation from Russian): "To Her Imperial Majesty Czarina Alexandra Feodorovna from the Iron-works Management and Dealers in the Siberian iron section of the Nijegorodski Fair in the year 1896."

Thus the room in the Winter Palace where Fabergé items were customarily held, continued to be filled with photo frames vying for attention among cigarette boxes and pen holders.

The fate of Nicholas is well known. On March 2, 1918 he was forced to abdicate following the revolution and a few months later, on July 17, he was shot with his entire family at Ekaterinburg. It was 80 years before the family were afforded a dignified burial in St Petersburg, with the doctor and servants who died alongside them.

It was through his links with the Russian royals that Fabergé achieved fame. But he did not work exclusively for them. He numbered the monarchs of other countries among his valued customers, especially England's King Edward VII. Indeed, staff at Fabergé's London outlet on 48 Dover Street, were compromised after both King Edward and Queen Alexandra insisted on viewing every new Fabergé item before anyone else

in order to choose a present for the other. To further complicate matters, courtiers were keen to buy gifts for both from Fabergé, and so were the King's mistresses.

English royals made their purchases at Fabergé's London shop, frequently slipping in from the street informally, although Bainbridge was sometimes summoned by King Edward to render private viewings of Fabergé art. The sales ledgers from the London shop provided essential information about Fabergé to art historians of later years. For example, a silver rhinoceros with mechanical movement bought by the Lord Chamberlain Earl Howe for England's Queen Alexandra on November 5, 1909 cost him £60, and 300 roubles to make. Leopold de Rothschild bought the gold, rock crystal and enamel Coronation Vase on April 12, 1911 for a mighty £430 when it cost 2,705 roubles to produce. In one year alone in London, 713 objects were sold including 91 cigarette cases, 71 miniature Easter eggs, 25 stone carvings and 23 picture frames.

Queen Alexandra was an ardent collector of Fabergé and voiced her hopes of one day meeting the master. In common with other royals she was used to people complying with her requests. Yet her hopes of meeting the craftsman were dashed when he fled from Britain rather than face this monarch and admirer. In 1908, Fabergé — rarely away from Russia — was delivering an item for the Queen to London when his assistant Bainbridge told him of the Queen's earnest desire. Whether from false modesty or genuine fear, Fabergé nervously, but determinedly declined. Nor did he wish to offend the Queen by prolonging his stay. Within 30 minutes of hearing this news, Fabergé was on a train heading for Paris.

When Queen Alexandra died in 1925 she was found to possess one of the largest collections of Fabergé then in existence. The English royal family still possess a tremendous array of Fabergé in personal collections bought then and later, for Queen Mary, wife of King George and daughter-in-law to Queen Alexandra, who likewise had a weakness for Fabergé.

Nature knows incomparable beauty. But Fabergé made a bold attempt to capture that breath-taking splendor and succeeded in a way that few craftsmen could.

Petals were not just finely shaped enamel. They bore veins as any real bloom would, no bigger than a hair's breadth. The leaves furled or spread much as real foliage might, a testament to the skill of the craftsman in his use of enamel, jade or nephrite. Fabergé's one concession to the goldsmith's craft was the subtle and delightful use of small stones on selected pieces. The flair of each lily of the valley flower was made from rose diamonds, the pansy had a brilliant diamond center, delicate japonica flowers dotted along a sprig each had small rose-diamond centers. There were branches and twigs of catkins, hawthorns, raspberries, cranberries and holly.

The flower studies have a certain rarity value. Although 10,000 items were sold through Fabergé's London outlet while it was open, only 35 were floral sprigs. Queen Alexandra of

127

England is said to have owned at least 20 of Fabergé's flower studies.

Even the experts can find difficulty in deciding which flowers were Fabergé's. Very few bear distinguishing marks.

In 1897, Fabergé was appointed as goldsmith to the court of the Swedish and Norwegian royal families.

The Siamese court (modern-day Thailand) were likewise beguiled by the work of Fabergé. In 1904, he was invited to visit the court of King Maha Chulongkorn whose son, Prince Chakrabongse, had been living and studying in Russia in the care of the Russian royals. The king had toured Fabergé's workshops in St Petersburg as early as 1897. It was for the King of Siam that Fabergé made a series of Buddha likenesses. Other items made for the Siamese royals were figures from Brahmin mythology, illustrating once again the versatility of the man and his corporation.

While Fabergé was undoubtedly fashionable it is worth remembering that his clients didn't see themselves as collectors or investors in works of art. They simply liked what they saw and made their purchases accordingly.

There were numerous other members of Europe's nobility who sought Fabergé toys and trinkets. Henry Bainbridge outlines the profile of the clientele when he relates the people he met during the course of his work as "ambassador" for the House of Fabergé:

"(I encountered) all the kings and all the queens, all the multi-millionaires, all the mandarins and all the maharajahs, all the dukes and all the marquises, all the earls, viscounts, barons and baronets."

**Below:** A beechwood frame embellished by the silver gilt Imperial crown at the top containing a photograph of the Grand Duchesses Olga, Tatiana, Maria, Anastasia and the Czarevitch Alexei, signed by them all.

**Above:** This is a *kovsh*, a drinking vessel originally carved from wood in the shape of a duck or goose. This one is made of nephrite and bears a large gold "A" on its handle. It was first bought by a member of the Spanish royal family.

**Above right**: A silver, enamel and gemset cigarette case given by Sophy de Torby as a gift in 1891, as the inscription reveals. The assumption is the present was for her husband-to-be Grand Duke Michael Michaelevich. Their daughter was Nada, who wed George Mountbatten.

**Right**: The family link continues with this gold mounted gemset silver cigarette case which is inscribed: "To dear Georgie with much love from Nada's parents."

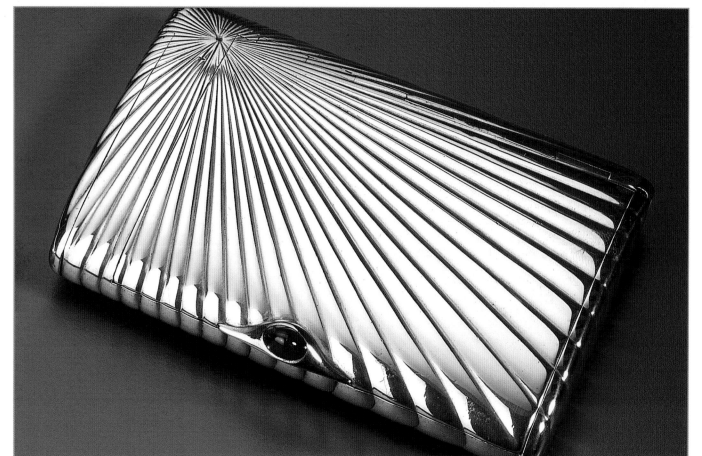

**Above:** Toadstool-style handseals made of rock crystal with rough caps and smooth stalks. Two of the five are marked on the base, one with an "M" below a crown, and the other "MCM" below a crown. It seems they once belonged to the Mordvinoff family in Russia. The largest is two and three eighths of an inch high.

**Above:** The royal connotations on this porcelain presentation vase made under the auspices of Julius Rappoport are clear to see. The entwined gilt cyphers of Czar Nicholas and his wife appear beneath an Imperial crown on its sides while the Romanov gryphon forms the top piece. Its presentation case stamped with Fabergé is made of oak.

**Left**: The magnificent clock made to commemorate the 25th wedding anniversary of Czar Alexander III and the Empress Marie presented in the fall of 1891 by 32 family members.

**SO WHAT BECAME OF FABERGÉ'S WORK**
**following the Russian Revolution when it was**
**no longer a commodity which could be**
**purchased across a glass counter in Russia or**
**London? Some had been sold abroad before**
**the First World War by Fabergé. Collectors**
**included wealthy American businessmen like**
**Henry C. Walters of Baltimore, probably the**
**first US buyer of Fabergé, when he made his**
**initial purchase in St Petersburg in 1900.**
**Millionaire J. Pierpont Morgan Walters Jr. also**
**added to his collection in 1930 when he bought**
**further items, including a gold latticed egg,**
**from Alexander Polovtsoff in the US. Julia**
**Grant, daughter of American general Ulysses S.**
**Grant, (US president from 1869–77), married**
**the eminent Russian Count Speransky to**
**become Princess Cantacuzene. After receiving**
**Fabergé gifts at her wedding, she also became**
**one of the early American collectors.**

American-born Consuelo Vanderbilt bought considerable quantities of Fabergé, before the Russian Revolution, from the company's London headquarters. The daughter of William and Alva Vanderbilt, she married the 9th Duke of Marlborough and was a cousin to British Prime Minister Winston Churchill. She was known as much for her great beauty as for her commitment to social welfare.

Her marriage was unhappy. Of her husband, Sunny, she wrote: "(He) was raised an unloved child. Like the others he was raised first by a nanny and then by boarding school masters. He spent little time with his parents in his formative years. British peers don't expect warm, embracing love within the family. Perhaps that is why they make such inferior husbands."

After 11 years, Consuelo quit the marriage and found happiness following her meeting, in 1921, French aviator Jacques Balsan. As a tireless campaigner for the disadvantaged, the Fabergé jewelry, which had adorned her at society balls and the like, soon became expendable and later joined the pieces in general circulation.

The fabulously wealthy Rothschild family were customers and collectors. Often gifts were bought for the Rothschilds in their racing colors, dark blue and yellow.

Stanislas Poklewski-Koziell, a counsellor at the Russian Embassy in London, was responsible for the distribution of numerous Fabergé articles before the revolution in Edwardian England. Typically, he would arrive at house parties on the country estates of the British nobility bearing suitcases full of Fabergé which he gave to the female hostess and guests.

But it is fair to assume that the majority of important pieces remained in Russia before the outbreak of the First World War. Some of the collection, including a number of the Fabergé eggs, were stored in the Hermitage, the treasury of the Winter Palace in St Petersburg, and in the Armoury Museum in the Kremlin. This collection was secure — for a while, at least.

**Previous page:** One of the largest eggs made by Fabergé. Please see page 38.

**Right:** Once the property of Julia Cantacuzene, daughter of US President Ulysses S. Grant, this rhodonite desk clock has a *guilloche* enameled face within a decorative gold and enamel band. It stands less than three inches in height.

In the chaos that ensued after the revolution, Fabergé artifacts were, like their creator, soon en route out of Russia. Some left in the possession of royal family members and Russian nobles who escaped the revolution and traveled to Europe or America. Many of these people quickly became hard-up and found that Fabergé pieces were a ready currency in countries that, until then, had for the most part been deprived of such artwork. Thus a channel was opened through which Fabergé items were released onto the open market. The flip side of this was that a previously restricted market was suddenly swamped and the desirability of Fabergé items dipped. It was reported in 1925 that Prince Youssoupoff, once the eminent Russian charmer, pawned what were reputedly Romanov family jewels in Berlin for about 60 per cent of their value. Just how many pieces were bought cheaply and melted down or broken up can only be guessed.

Clearly, the bejeweled items in the property of the Russian royals were an anathema to the Bolsheviks who eschewed such frippery.

Government is a costly business and it was made more so for the Bolsheviks through an international blockade on trade imposed by former war-time allies. Still, the infant regime found itself in the happy position of being able to raise money by selling Fabergé paraphernalia to foreigners. Much of it was sold by the weight rather than by the item. In this way, many Fabergé items were dispersed across the world. Of course, this treatment wasn't reserved solely for Fabergé and applied to Russian art across the board. The extent of the sell-off, which occured mostly between 1927 and 1938, has only become clear since the fall of Communism which has allowed art historians to view government records.

In turn, the Americans were fascinated by the tragedy of the Czars and an enthusiastic market was generated.

Paving the way for the market between the two countries was Dr. Armand Hammer. New York-born Hammer was the son Dr. Julius Hammer — the first card-carrying member of the US Communist Labour Party. Julius allegedly named his son symbolically in honor of the worker's cause (arm-and-hammer).

Armand enjoyed a personal rapport with Lenin which initially facilitated the trade of Fabergé items. He continued to bring artifacts out of Russia and found a market even when the Western world was in the grips of the Great Depression. With a traveling exhibition of Fabergé items he made converts across America.

In 1956, he won control of the Occidental Petroleum company, underlining his personal wealth. Following his death he has been accused of being a Communist spy and traitor. Whether or not this is true, he brought considerable quantities of the art of Fabergé out of Russia before the Iron Curtain descended, after which the remainder was veiled from millions of admirers.

Two of the pre-eminent buyers after the war were the oil magnate Calouste Sarkis Gulbenkian (1869–1955) who bought directly from the Hermitage in St Petersburg and Andrew Mellon (1855–1937), US Secretary of the Treasury under three presidents and renown philanthropist. His extensive art collection was left to the American people and can be seen in the Washington National Gallery of Art.

There were some notable individual collectors. Marjorie Merriweather Post (1887–1973) was one. The daughter of a food manufacturing millionaire, she was taught everything she would ever need to know about business practise by him before his death in 1914.

Her knowledge of the fine arts was largely self taught. Appreciation of the arts became such a major feature in her life that she eventually signed up for classes at the Metropolitan Museum of Art.

She was married three times, lastly to Joseph E. Davies, who was the American Ambassador to the Soviet Union between 1937 and 1938. She was horrified by the harsh extremes of Stalin's rule. But she witnessed first hand how economic necessity forced the regime to sell off still more of its heritage.

Ironically Marjorie did not buy any of the 90 pieces in her collection at his time although her 18 months spent in Russia served to strengthened her love of Russian art. She acquired her Fabergé purchases following their export to America.

Her collection — at one time the largest of Russia Imperial art outside the mother country — included copious examples of Fabergé's work including an ornate table clock once the property of the Dowager Empress Marie, and was ultimately bequeathed to the public. At her request Hillwood, her home in Washington DC, was turned into a museum stocked with her personal items.

In 1947, Lillian Thomas Pratt, of Fredericksburg, bequeathed her impressive collection of Fabergé items to the Virginia Museum of Fine Arts, including four Imperial eggs — the Pelican Egg of 1897; the Peter the Great egg of 1903; the Czarevich Egg of 1912, and the Rock Crystal Egg of 1896. Her generosity left the museum boasting the largest collection of Imperial eggs outside Russia.

Matilda Geddings Gray left her personal Fabergé collection in the care of the New Orleans Area Museum.

India Early Minshall (1885–1965) was born and brought up in Columbus, Ohio, in a wealthy, well-established family. After marrying petroleum executive Thaddeus Ellis Minshall she settled in Cleveland. Together they reveled in books about pre-Revolutionary Russia. Only after his death in 1930 did India indulge herself further by buying Russian artworks, specifically those made by Fabergé.

Her first Fabergé items was a small clock bought in 1937 from the Hammer Galleries for $250. She continued to acquire Fabergé artifacts with zeal, culminating in the purchase of the Red Cross Egg for $4,400 in 1943. When she died she bequeathed her collection of about 60 Fabergé items to the Cleveland Museum. Curator Henry H. Hawley revealed: "Though not of enormous size, Minshall's Fabergé collection include representative examples of every significant variety of object that Fabergé made. It is the remarkable degree of concurrence of historic importance, technical quality and beauty of the particular pieces that makes this Fabergé collection a distinguished one."

Fascinated by the story of the Czars, American publisher Malcolm S. Forbes bought his wife a Fabergé cigarette box for Christmas during a visit to London. It was the beginning of a lifelong passion. He pulled together the *Forbes* Magazine collection after having purchased significant amounts of Fabergé from collectors Jack and Belle Linsky via Helen and Lansdell K. Christie, the shipping magnate. The *Forbes* Magazine collection in New York includes these eggs: the Rosebud Egg of 1895; The Coronation Egg of 1897; the Lilies of the Valley Egg of 1898; the Chanticleer Egg of 1903 and the Fifteenth Anniversary Egg of 1911.

A sizeable collection remains in the hands of the British royal family. The Queen Mother, the Queen, Princess Margaret, Princess Anne and the Duke of Gloucester all possess Fabergé pieces, as does the Prince of Wales.

Intriguingly, in 1997 an Italian cat burglar, Renato Rinino, claimed to have raided St James' Palace three years previously and taken Fabergé cufflinks encrusted with rose diamonds, sapphires and rubies which were once the property of Czar Nicholas II. The thief claims to have returned the stolen items and has promised to write a book about his adventures.

Lady Zia (Anastasia), a great granddaughter of Czar Nicholas I, accrued a collection of Fabergé items at her stately home, Luton Hoo, in Bedfordshire before her death in 1977 at the age of 84. She was married to Sir Harold Wernher, heir to the fortune made by his father Sir Julius in the diamond mines of Kimberley, South Africa.

Comedienne Joan Rivers is one of today's most enthusiastic collectors.

Two of the best known companies dealing in Fabergé were — and are — À La Vieille Russie in America and Wartski's in London.

À La Vieille Russie (ALVR) began in Kiev, Russia, in 1851 when Gustav Fabergé was at work in St Petersburg. With the onset of the Russian Revolution it moved from Kiev to Paris. As the Second World War approached it migrated again, this time to New York where it has remained, its famous shop front adorning Fifth Avenue. Best known of it managers was Jacques Zolotnitzky. It was ALVR that sold six of the Fabergé Kelch eggs to a private American collector after purchasing them from a French jeweller who himself bought them from Mrs Kelch in 1920.

Wartski of Llandudno was founded in 1865 by Morris Wartski, an immigrant from Bohemia. Wartski first began trading in Bangor, North Wales, but moved to Llandudno on the advice of lawyer David Lloyd George, before the latter became Britain's war-time Prime Minister. The venue was well-starred. Britain's rich and famous flocked to Llandudno, one of the most fashionable resorts of Victorian times.

Morris Wartski was replaced as chairman by Emanuel Snowman, who had married Wartski's daughter Harriet in 1910. It was Snowman who opened a branch of the business on Grafton Street in London's West End, frustrated as he was by life in rural Wales.

Emanuel began making trips to Russia during the troubled years of the First World War and the revolution. He seized his opportunities, buying Russian antiques and a variety of Fabergé items. His son Kenneth remembers being told not to touch a purchase residing temporarily in the family home in north west London. It was one of the Imperial Easter eggs.

Kenneth pursued a career in the art world in his younger days. He exhibited at the Royal Academy and worked both as a children's book illustrator and, after 1939, a war artist. However, he joined the family firm in 1940 following his marriage and became a confirmed admirer of Fabergé items. He has since become an expert on the genre and is recognized as such the world over.

Wartski's continues to enjoy close links with the British royals and displays the "By Royal Appointment" crest.

Collectors are also familiar with the name of French firm Lacloche Frères which had been buying Fabergé items since the turn of the century and bought up the unsold stock held for Fabergé in London when Bainbridge stopped trading.

The business of forgery has always flourished. A concern, since Fabergé, with its exclusivity and ability to command high prices, attracts fakery in droves. Take the study of certain flowers, for example, it is almost impossible to mark them sufficiently well so that they cannot be convincingly copied. So it is difficult even for the experts to differentiate between genuine Fabergé and items similarly designed and made. These and small items, like stone carvings, are those most likely to be mimicked.

Confusion arises for various reasons. Sometimes the name "Fabergé" is added alongside the maker's name in the belief it will increase an item's value. This may also be done in the conviction that a piece of Russian art did indeed emerge from the Fabergé workshops and it is stamped so it can rightfully join the fold. In fact, many of the Fabergé items were stamped before completion. Unlike the fakes, the stamp is then flush with the metal. Replicas of Fabergé art were being made as early as 1900 and such imitations have a certain value of their own.

The poorly made replica does not fool folk for long. But in these days of advanced technology it has become easier than ever before to re-create the fine lines of a piece of art made years before. Experts can then be duped into believing an item is genuine.

Even before the days of technological wizardry there were credible forgeries in circulation. It has been mooted that luminaries such as Dr. Armand Hammer and even Carl's sons Eugene and Alexander Fabergé have engineered the production of fakes during the Soviet era. The former was allegedly supervising work in Soviet Russia while the latter operated in Paris.

Experts in Russia have the advantage as they can work from archive records, dating back to when Fabergé was in business. Notwithstanding it is alleged that an egg bearing the marks of Victor Aarne, the Fabergé silversmith, was bought in good faith by the State Museum in Moscow during the 1980s and turned out to be a fake.

Once the myth is accepted as fact in the higher echelons of the art world, and published in books and catalogs as such, it is hard to assert the truth. Collectors, too, are equally vulnerable. When they are convinced about a piece it is impossible to sway them, not least because they would be seriously out of pocket if their possession was exposed as a fraud.

Still De Tiesenhausen from Christie's does not view the issue of Fabergé forgery as particularly pressing:

"The Fabergé collectors are in a very small club and they are very discreet. It is a specialised, small field. Forgery has always occured — and not just with Fabergé. You need a number of years of experience to be right-footed. People love to talk about it as a matter of sensation. It is a problem but not a huge problem."

If in doubt, it is better to buy from a dealer with a proven track record who shows no disinclination to trade again with stock from which he has already parted.

As for the Fabergé family, tradition continues with Theo, son of Nicholas and grandson of Carl. Born in 1922, Theo crafted items as a hobby using a lathe dating from 1861. Only after he sold his successful engineering company in 1974 could he turn his attention to producing artworks full time. Since then he has produced a variety of items — even eggs similar in concept to those which made the family name famous. Although an Englishman by nationality his work has been seen in Russia. In 1988 he was asked to design a millenium egg for the Russian Orthodox Church. A previous commission by the Church — exiled under Communist rule — was to his grandfather. And in 1995 he presented The Moscow Egg to the Hermitage Museum in St Petersburg.

**Above:** Workmasters on this Fabergé piece, used gold, silver, platinum, diamonds, pearls, and sapphires to recreate a perfect miniature of the Imperial regalia.

**THE APPEAL OF FABERGÉ HAS NOT DIMINISHED WITH TIME. A new century is upon us and still the fascination with the jewelry, the eggs, the figures and figurines and the rest remains as strong as ever.**

In 1996 two exhibitions "Fabergé in America" and "The Lillian Thomas Pratt Collection of Fabergé" were on view at the Virginia Museum of Fine Arts in the US. It featured 15 Imperial eggs and some 400 other Fabergé pieces. The 12-week show attracted 130,000 visitors. Between them they spent an estimated 3.6 million dollars on food, lodging and other purchases in addition to the 600,000 dollars raised in ticket sales. So the impact to Richmond, Virginia — one of five venues for the exhibition in America — was phenomenal. In an era when the arts are deemed an intolerable drain on resources it is hardly surprising that Fabergé should once again be setting the trends.

142

**Right:** The Pine Cone Egg.
see pages 35 and 36

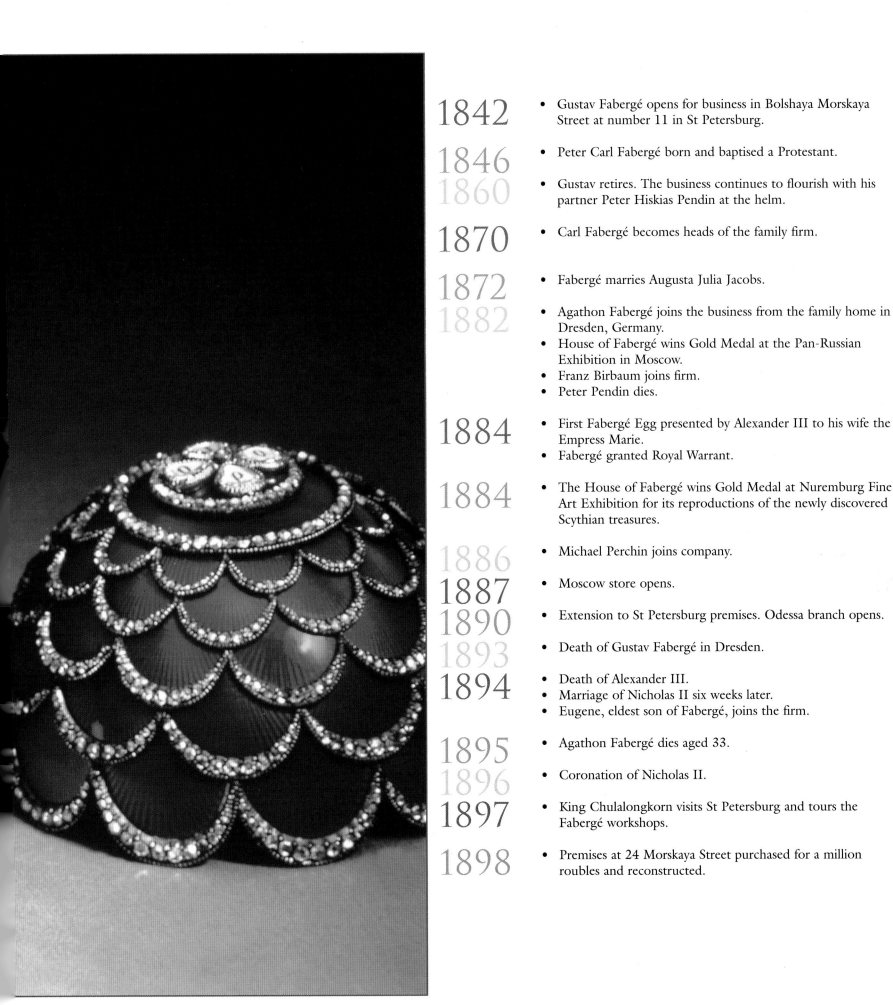

**1842** • Gustav Fabergé opens for business in Bolshaya Morskaya Street at number 11 in St Petersburg.

**1846** • Peter Carl Fabergé born and baptised a Protestant.

**1860** • Gustav retires. The business continues to flourish with his partner Peter Hiskias Pendin at the helm.

**1870** • Carl Fabergé becomes heads of the family firm.

**1872** • Fabergé marries Augusta Julia Jacobs.

**1882** • Agathon Fabergé joins the business from the family home in Dresden, Germany.
• House of Fabergé wins Gold Medal at the Pan-Russian Exhibition in Moscow.
• Franz Birbaum joins firm.
• Peter Pendin dies.

**1884** • First Fabergé Egg presented by Alexander III to his wife the Empress Marie.
• Fabergé granted Royal Warrant.

**1884** • The House of Fabergé wins Gold Medal at Nuremburg Fine Art Exhibition for its reproductions of the newly discovered Scythian treasures.

**1886** • Michael Perchin joins company.

**1887** • Moscow store opens.

**1890** • Extension to St Petersburg premises. Odessa branch opens.

**1893** • Death of Gustav Fabergé in Dresden.

**1894** • Death of Alexander III.
• Marriage of Nicholas II six weeks later.
• Eugene, eldest son of Fabergé, joins the firm.

**1895** • Agathon Fabergé dies aged 33.

**1896** • Coronation of Nicholas II.

**1897** • King Chulalongkorn visits St Petersburg and tours the Fabergé workshops.

**1898** • Premises at 24 Morskaya Street purchased for a million roubles and reconstructed.

143

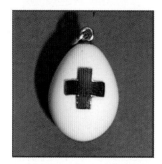

**1900**
- Morskaya Street becomes Fabergé headquarters.
- Imperial eggs, loaned by the Dowager Empress and Czarina, go on display at the Paris "Exposition Internationale Universelle" and help Fabergé to win international acclaim, including the coveted Cross of the Legion of Honour.

**1901**
- Erik Kollin dies.

**1903**
- Fabergé goes on sale in London at Berners Hotel.
- Michael Perchin dies, as does August Hollstrom.

**1904**
- Tsarevitch is born.
- Fabergé items go on display at the Royal Albert Hall in London in a fund raising bazaar for a children's hospital organized by Lady Arthur Paget.

**1905**
- Kiev branch opens.

**1906**
- London branch opens at 48 Dover Street.

**1908**
- Fabergé makes fleeting visit to London.

**1910**
- Kiev branch closes.
- Fabergé loses a high court battle to prevent the English import mark from being added to the pieces he sold through London.

**1911**
- London branch moves to 173 New Bond Street.

**1914**
- Outbreak of First World War. Fabergé's company and its craftsmen are compelled to make small arms for soldiers.

**1915**
- Bond Street shop closes. August Hollming dies.

**1916**
- Julius Rappoport dies.

**1917**
- Russian Revolution.

**1918**
- House of Fabergé closed down by Bolsheviks.
- Murder of the Czar and his family. Empress Marie is exiled, first to England before settling in her native Denmark.
- Fabergé poses as courier attached to the British embassy to flee Russia via Riga and Berlin.

**1920**
- Fabergé settles in Lausanne but dies soon afterwards.

**1925**
- Augusta Fabergé dies in Cannes.

**1929**
- Eugene inters the remains of his father in Cannes with those of his mother.